A Zen Companion
In a Just and Effective Classroom

2nd Edition

Mike Bergsgaard

D1416139

ICIE
THE INTERNATIONAL CENTRE FOR
INNOVATION IN EDUCATION

International Contact:
Taisir Subhi Yamin, General Director
Heilmeyersteige 93, D-89075, Ulm, Germany.
Email: taisir@icieworld.net
Ph: (+49)172-929-7632

Canadian Contact:
Kari McCluskey, Regional Director
Box 111, Domain, Manitoba, R0G 0M0
Email: ka.mccluskey@lostprizes.com

URL: www.icieworld.net

Cover Photo: Mike Bergsgaard

Printed in Canada

ISBN: 978-0-9917929-4-8

MIX
Paper from
responsible sources
FSC www.fsc.org **FSC® C016245**

Acknowledgments

I wish to express my thanks to all of those with whom
I've shared a classroom for the unique and enlightening
ways in which we've brought each other into being.

My appreciation to
The University of Winnipeg
for sustenance and opportunity.

A Zen Companion
(in a Just and Effective Classroom)

A well-meant word of clarification: this is not a guide; it is not a recipe; it may not be easily accessible simply because it purports to be neither. It may require thinking and feeling and it will not tell you how to do either. It is resistant to speed reading and third-party plot summaries. It is challenging and it makes demands upon the reader's time, patience, and intelligence just as being in the "Just and Effective" classroom has often proven to make the same demands upon the instructor and students (and I apply those labels to the people "in the room" only for clarification and not with regard to status). Engaging with this narrative may be similar to the following description of a lock being picked (which we would do also only out of necessity – or curiosity):

"All you had to do was line up those pins just right so the thing could turn freely ... then, finally, the really interesting part. The absolutely most fascinating and satisfying part of all, how I could put a little bit of tension on that cylinder. ... I could push up each pin, one by one, letting the tension keep them in place as I moved on to the next, until finally all five pins were lined up perfectly. How the lock, without the use of a key, would then slide smoothly and magically open. ... When you finally open it. ... When you finally learn how to unlock the lock ... can you even imagine how that feels?" (Hamilton, 2009, p. 37)

Further, if you involve your Self entirely with the following, you will know no more at that point than you do at this moment; you may, however, be more aware of just how much you already do know.

When I was first asked by a colleague to provide a resource that would serve as a guide to others intending to replicate the Just and Effective Schools course which I developed for the Faculty of Education and have subsequently taught more than a dozen times, my response was that it was impossible to distill the ineffable. Moreover, if the course can be viewed as an organic entity, it was not originally created as an exemplary template to inform all future inquiries; rather it was conceived as being a collective, evolving, and unscripted quest for the pure light of truth in the classroom and in the minds of those in that space.

My colleague, however, was quietly insistent that, if not distilled, the "ineffable" could be "represented;" consequently, what I endeavor to do in this discussion, is to offer to the reader "a memory" with thoughts and alternative observations that contain the key features of this course as it has unfolded in its various manifestations in order to represent for the reader the experience of "being" in a Just and Effective classroom.

The account offered here is contextualized in a representation of actual events compressed from the different sections of the course as well as in the more salient experiences of that first group of intrepid and trusting students in the original Just and Effective Schools class. It recreates, as precisely as I recall, the daily dialectic and natural praxis as both have commonly unfolded during those three-month courses in the decade leading up to this writing. To add dimension and validity to the narrative, I include student comments from our classes, excerpts from informal conversations with students, and written contributions from two former students: Details of the last days of the first course offered in 2001 are written by James Tyson, one of many keen thinkers and good beings in that group; and, interspersed throughout this reconstruction and juxtaposed with the commentary on the first course, are insights written by Laura Davey, a member of the recent 2011 class and a clear-thinking, curious, and courageous seeker on her own journey. In addition to enhancing the discussion by adding Laura's thoughts, the purpose in placing her comments in proximity to events occurring in the first Just and Effective course a decade earlier is to give the reader a more immediate sense of constants across the courses as well as the unpredictable variables.

As I detail throughout, there was no exact direction available to me when I first conceived of the course, and as the reader will see, there is rarely a precise direction that I, or the students will take on a given day in any given moment. To convey that "ineffable" but indispensable element of the course, I have written what follows in the manner in which a Just and

Effective class characteristically unfolds. At times the narrative may seem to lack consistency and predictability, but that is the essence of the interaction that is common to this particular course. For instance, I begin the "distillation" by recounting a minor incident, which actually took place recently when I was running outdoors. I include this because, across the span of any given Just and Effective course, I very commonly draw upon everyday events in my life to explore the ideas we are discussing and I encourage students to contribute from their daily experiences as well. The reader will also notice, perhaps with some irritation, that I have inserted quotations, comments, or elaborations that depart from the narrative thread.

Like this: **You are my Self as the Other; I am your Self in the form of the Other.**

Again, I do so because where those ideas are broached in this discussion, they likewise often occur to me in the temporal unfolding of an actual class. I include these tangential asides not only with the hope that they may invite thought and feeling in the reader, but also to serve as a guide to the reader hoping to understand the thought and feeling that go into the course from moment to moment. Where these inserts are the exclusive expressions of others, I have credited those sources appropriately. Where inserts are simply recorded in bold type, these are ideas which I have actually had while teaching this course at those junctures indicated or they are ideas which have evoked the discussion following each (and please be advised that unlike like conventional guides, the inserts in this account may complement *or contradict* the idea being discussed). Clearly, the ideas which you have and when you have them will depend upon the reality you bring into being through your unique self. In what will appear to be ironical if not contradictory at this point, I offer this observation from St. Augustine: **"Don't go outside yourself, return into yourself. The dwelling place of truth is in the inner man" (Jackson, 1974, p. 177).** Now, if you understand completely the preceding quotation, and may impart that understanding at will, further engagement with this discussion may be unnecessary for you – or perhaps even more necessary.

Oh, and one more small matter. Wittgenstein (2009) has asserted that **"Philosophy is a struggle against the bewitchment of our understanding by the resources of our language" (p. 52).** For our current purposes, we must agree to consider language to be as much a risk as it is a vehicle for understanding what we already know.

"... ideologies, beliefs, opinions, and points of view, not to mention the factual knowledge accumulated since birth (to which we attach ourselves), are the shadows which obscure the light of truth" (Kapleau, 1989, p. 32).

Student: This course is entitled "The Just and Effective School."

What is a just school?

Instructor: It may depend on who you ask and when.

Student: I'm asking you now.

Instructor: Then you may be looking further than you have to and in the wrong direction.

To the reader: What to you at this moment is one absolute static truth? What do you "know" before you begin thinking? Is it not that you are? What do you know as certainly after that point? What do these questions have to do with "just" schools?

The Beginning – A lifetime in every moment:

Rather than accepting that existence precedes essence, I would suggest that existence is essence; we just don't appreciate our moment-to-moment lives that way. For instance, this small matter in the cosmic stream: I am jogging along a familiar neighborhood route before sunrise. It is quiet – little traffic. Suddenly I sense motion to my left and behind me … then a frantic barking and a shadow rushing low toward my ankles. A woman's voice beseeches, "No, come back here! Get back here!" I look down to locate the dog, which has now abandoned its pursuit and turned to face its owner.

The Heisenberg uncertainty principle … "suggested that the consciousness of the observer brought the observed object into being. Nothing in the universe existed as an actual thing independently of our observation of it. Every minute of every day we were creating our own world" (McTaggart, 2008, p. 12).

A minor interaction; one of countless others in any given day in anyone's life anywhere in the world. However minor it may be, though, the way in which I experience the event, the way in which I react in the midst of it, the way I will think about it is a representation of all that I am and all that has gone before me. All time, space, and events converge on that moment and I bring it all into being through my being. My feelings about the dog, my thoughts about the animal, my interaction with its owner, my sense of who was right or who was wrong may be described in Ezra Pounds' (1918) words from "A Retrospect" "as an intellectual and emotional complex in an instant of time;" it is the same for the dog and it is the same for the master. But how much of that event will I really understand? What did I feel and when did I feel it? Did I respond out of a thoughtfully constructed model of justice or did I simply act out of a primal sense of preservation? I offer this scenario not only to animate the intention of this discussion, which is the inquiry into the Self to locate forms of truth, but also to suggest that many of the moments that constitute our lives are not understood, felt, or appreciated.

Please allow me to be more specific to clarify what I mean before we go further into why there might be some worth in you reading this. When running, I am usually in a state of alertness. It is something I have been doing for half my life and I've learned that turning on to an open pathway may open up a beautiful stretch of scenery or reveal a car coming straight for me while the driver is busily texting. **If the medium is the message, then the body is the penultimate statement ... !**

When I first caught sight of the approaching dog in the scenario just recounted, my alertness escalated into fear in an instant. Fear of being hurt, fear of being humiliated, fear of the next moment. I didn't have to explore my store of memories – the sight of the dog seemed to provoke those recollections whether of being bitten or having a friendly pup unintentionally trip me up. I don't recall thinking of each memory, but we usually don't. We are wired to flee, freeze, or fight but the antecedent to each is fear. Fear – undetected fear is the backdrop to all classrooms – indoors or outside. It may be as Parker Palmer (1998) claims: **"Fear is what distances us from our colleagues, our students, our subjects, ourselves. Fear shuts down those 'experiments with truth' that allow us to weave a wider web of consciousness"** (p. 36). Inside or outside, fear just appears so quickly we don't think about where it came from.

"Rarely do we question our strategies, which are always rooted in fear. We believe in them as the unquestioned truth ... consequently, our life narrows down to a sense of vague dissatisfaction" (Bayda, 2002, p. 3).

So – to "flee, freeze, or fight." I detect the shadow moving swiftly toward me and options – most based upon my life experiences – fortuitously flash before me (and here we see the relationship between rich experience and choice and understand why those lacking the first often have less of the second). Run faster? Kick the animal? I do neither but stop. The fear begins to subside. Why? The master's voice. I know from experience – although I don't focus on that memory exactly – that where an owner intercedes, the dog is less likely to cause harm. Sure enough, the amiable golden retriever begins to blithely lick my shoe as though that was his only intention from the outset. Now, however, the fear is displaced by anger, which is almost always the product of thought. Why wasn't this beast on a leash as the law requires? What kind of a person allows a dog to rush into the street at risk to itself, a passing runner, or a texting driver? How can I trust this person? This dog? Not only is this owner flaunting the law, she is also ignoring the most basic principles of good citizenship and morality. I am entitled to point out to her the incorrectness in her behavior. In fact, I may have a duty to correct her and her animal or the two of them will be making a habit of these egregious breaches in common civility.

"In order to express your anger, you have to justify it to yourself first. You have to convince yourself that anger is deserved, appropriate, right. In the mental process that is anger, it is as if a trial occurs in your mind" (Brahm, 2005, p. 73).

But then she interrupts my inquiry into justness and offers, "I am so sorry ... he just slipped off his leash ... we're watching him for our neighbors." Ah-ha, well, okay, that may serve as an acceptable excuse for your error. The anger now gives way to a feeling of "connection" and empathy – the poor woman isn't at fault and the dog was just doing what dogs do naturally. "Quite all right, no harm done – have a nice day." And I go happily on my way, the dog seeks out other malodorous targets and the owner, I presume, has learned her lesson. I'm happy with that outcome and decide that, the next time I come under scrutiny from a dog, I'll use the same strategy. And there was no lingering hostility – it was a decent human interaction unlike those conflicts where one spends the rest of the day replaying the event, trying to imagine more creative and insulting paybacks, then fearing that the other person was also contriving more effective plans for revenge.

Two monks are watching a flag. One observes, "The flag is moving." The other counters, "The wind is moving." A passerby kindly offers, "Not the wind, not the flag. Mind is moving." (Traditional Zen Commentary)

Now this has been considerable writing and reading to distill one ten-second incident, but I hope that it demonstrates the emotional and intellectual complexity that is a defining feature of our lives. Moreover, I hope that it hints at my contention, that all of us have elaborate and dynamic views of what is "just' depending upon our past experience, our prevailing mood, the players involved in a scenario, and a multitude of other variables we will look at further into our journey. Said simply, it is quite likely that most of us, most of the time, live those unexamined lives that Plato warned against. **For many of us, the stranger with whom we spend the most time is our own Self.** We don't really know what each of us believes justice to be; we construct an idea out of it from borrowed notions, we base it upon principles indoctrinated into us, and we act out of it as though it was an immutable truth of the universe despite an abiding and unsettling understanding that, if challenged on the term, we couldn't explain why our version of justice was any more superior or correct than the justice of a child soldier fighting under the tutelage and coercion of an immoral war lord. If justice is that relative, if it is that elusive, how then do we begin to define, let alone create a just and effective school? Allow me to share with you a detailed account of these challenges we have encountered and learned from in our efforts to bring into being that interaction known in our university as "Just and Effective Schools."

"The true understanding is that the mind includes everything; when you think something comes from outside it means only that something appears in your mind. Nothing outside your mind can cause you any trouble" (Suzuki, 1990, p. 34).

With the evolution of the Faculty of Education at the University of Winnipeg from a four-year to a five-year degree, it was necessary to develop courses which would be of value to pre-service teachers and also meet the Faculty's mandate for educating students to teach in diverse settings but, in particular, the inner city. Toward this end, it was suggested at one of innumerable staff meetings across a span of eight years that we offer a course entitled "Just and Effective Schools." Quite confident that I had a general, if not clear, sense of what a just and effective school would be, and equally certain that I would never have to teach it anyway, I heartily endorsed the proposal if for no other reason than to expedite closure of the meeting.

Six years later, I was choked with fear, humbled by ignorance, and overcome with indignation at whomever had suggested the notion when I learned that my teaching load for the next year would require me to develop three new courses including something called "Just and Effective Schools."

"The new and the unformulated are exactly those realms where the aesthetics of wonder and other strong experiences of the unexpected, the unplaceable, the radically new are necessary guides to attention, curiosity, and the process of creating intelligibility" (Fisher, 1998, p. 144).

"Enrichment and Talent Development" I would be doing in concert with an experienced and gifted colleague – indeed, the very sentient and occasionally prescient soul who encouraged me to write this offering. "Topics in Inner City Schools" seemed challenging but manageable with the background and contacts I had in inner-city education, but this "Just and Effective Schools" suddenly seemed to be but a conundrum into which I would have a summer to work myself into and a term to work myself out of. The horror emerged from the realization that I had been a teacher or administrator in a number of settings all of which, to varying degrees, were just or effective; however none of which, by consensus, were always, or even often, both. This angst was exacerbated by my awareness that, aside from the credit hours, students might well choose this elective with the expectation that they would leave the course prepared to go forth to find (or worse yet, replicate) the definitive just and effective school detailed by me in twelve classes. Clearly, my first obligation was to search the continent for the just and effective school. Surely, I reasoned, someone somewhere had gone before me and blazed a trail to the Shangri-la of schools.

"A mother's letter to her son, a scholar:

There is no end to information and commentation, glory and honor. I wish you to stop this lecture business. Shut yourself up in a little temple in a remote part of the mountain. Devote your time to meditation and in this way attain true realization" (in Reps, 1961, p. 24).

I turned firstly to the literature and, not unexpectedly, found an abundance of research and thought on what defined and constituted not only an effective school but an effective teacher, effective administrator, even effective students. Although many of these statements were tempting and persuasive, none appeared to reconcile the dilemma created by the subjective nature of the terminology: Effective from whose perspective? Good from whose perspective? Ineffective from whose frame of reference? Perhaps, after thirty years in education, I had slipped into the trough of cynicism I had pledged I would avoid, but with every book and article I read, I could hear clearly the voice of a student, parent, teacher, administrator, or opposing author proclaim "Effective for you maybe, but not for me!" To confound the matter, I still hadn't done so much with the word "just" as looking it up in the dictionary.

"... school success is closely related to the degree to which the culture of the home corresponds with the culture of the school. Each child brings to school knowledge, values, skills and dispositions that are acquired outside of the school, primarily through her or his family interactions. This cultural capital ... is differentially valued and rewarded by the school system, with schools possessing a systemic preference for dominant white, middle-class male values, language, and views of the world. The consequence of this world view is that children's school experiences vary greatly ... [depending upon the degree to which the cultural capital of the home corresponds with that of the school]" (Young & Levin, 2002, p. 248).

The most grievous aspect of this dynamic is that no one in the school informs the child of this relationship so it is left to her or him to conclude that all success and failure is the result of intelligence and industry. Thus, "the myth of the meritocracy," as Samuel Bowles (1971) has termed it.

Is this "Just?" Perhaps for some ...

Is this "Effective?" Perhaps for some ...

Maybe I was climbing up a mountain most easily walked around; maybe someone in academe undertaking the same mission had already cracked the conundrum, created the course, and was willing to share. Quickly I engaged a most "effective" researcher and humbly requested that she scour the western hemisphere for any course which not only dealt with the topic but resolved the dilemma (in retrospect, perhaps we were scouring the wrong hemisphere, but funding was limited and it's tough to reach anyone east of England during the day). Despite her diligence and my urgings, we came across many wonderful courses being taught by many erudite people but failed to find what we were seeking (which, I hasten to add, doesn't mean it's not out there).

By midsummer, I had two tables mounded with books, pages of notes from our research, an absurdly vague course description in the University Calendar, but no course and no idea what to do about it. The only option seemed to be to concede the impossibility of constructing the impossible, confess the futility of my quest to the Dean, and ask that the course either be canceled or placed in the hands of someone more capable or less obsessed with semantics. In the meanwhile I would return to my work concerning the way in which the Contemplative Practitioner deconstructs the artificialities of the classroom. (Contemplative Practice was then in the incipient stages of development as a sanctioned practice in education but is founded in ancient thinking espoused in countless sources.)

"... contemplation, then is the state of consciousness where we are deeply attentive and often experience a sense of awe and wonder" (Miller, 1994, p. 4).

Although not ancient, Robert Pirsig's (1974) *Zen and the Art of Motorcycle Maintenance* is a timeless work to which I referred often not only for enjoyment but also for guidance in Contemplative thinking, particularly on the matter of how we define Quality and quality as well as the role of referential analogues in that process. It was while reading a passage by Pirsig to distract me from the impending confession I would be offering to the Dean that I had one of those rare moments of instantaneous insight that lit the path and provided a direction; it said, "let the truth tell itself." **In an age when information is as immediately accessible as the nearest laptop, the greatest, sometimes the only contribution a teacher can make is to think.**

At this point I will pause to tell you a story. When I was in the fourth grade my class was at recess where the boys were playing basketball and the girls were playing on the swings. As I was dribbling the ball forward on the asphalt playground this fine spring morning I was suddenly struck by the profound understanding that I was me and no one else was. I recall pausing momentarily and looking at the Other children. Up to that moment, I assumed we all shared in a collective knowing and understanding. In an instant I realized I had no idea what was happening in the heads of the Others and the Other did not really know me. Never had I felt so alone; never had I been so frightened. From that time forward, life was a process of re-connecting with the Other while holding on to my Self.

St. Augustine: "Man, though he feels lonely, is always in encounter with himself. The more he presses this dialogue of the self, the deeper he goes into the self itself. Sooner or later he encounters the Totally Other within the Self" (Jackson, 1974, p. 204).

During the first class I distributed the standard course outlines detailing assignments and grading schemes along with a compilation of articles and extracts. Sequentially, these works included an article by Bhandari (2000) on Plato's concept of justice, excerpts from *Zen and the Art of Motorcycle Maintenance* (Pirsig, 1974), Chapter 4 from Russell's (2000) *From Science to God*, *Pedagogy of the Oppressed* (Freire, 1970), an article by Shrewsbury (1987) on feminist pedagogy, a chapter from *Teaching to Transgress* by bell hooks (1994), and excerpts from *The Schools Our Children Deserve: Moving Beyond Traditional Classrooms and Tougher Standards* (Kohn, 1999).

After the perfunctory review of the course outline and before turning to the literature, I made a quick reference to the title of the course, suggested that we explore the characteristics of an "effective" school to begin with, then invited comments from the students. Within fifteen minutes, the class generated a list of at least a dozen features of an effective school; within the next fifteen minutes we uncovered a perspective which stood in opposition to each characteristic of an effective school. For example, although most adults and students in the school may perceive "respect" as being a matter of concern and regard for others, there may be some who view respect as a matter of instilling fear for the purposes of control. In another instance, one student argued that effective teachers treat all students the same; a classmate countered that each student is unique and needs to be treated according to his/her individual needs. What we tentatively concluded from this introductory exercise is that people will hold different opinions about what an effective school is, that each is legitimate, and that – very likely – there is no one school that all observers would agree is just or effective (notwithstanding claims to the contrary on school websites). Despite the relative nature of these terms, please notice below how even a commentator as respected as William Glasser (1998) writes with conviction and authority about "good" and "quality" as absolute truths which he has derived:

"*Good* students want grades because they represent *good* pay for *good* work (p. 108). ...Where a *quality school* would differ substantially from a traditional school is that only the courses in which students had done *quality work* would be recorded on their transcript" [italics added] (p. 110).

At this juncture, I suggested that our struggle with "just and effective" was very similar to the difficulty which Pirsig (1974) experienced in defining Quality before he concluded that quality is "... made up of what you know. It's an analogue to what you already know. It has to be ... it can't be anything else" (p. 317). I then told a story about inviting a group of junior high students to view a piece of sculpture that appeared to be a decrepit, rusting desk discarded in front of the university. In even the most charitable view, the students regarded the "art" as junk. Although I shared their assessment, I suggested that perhaps the sculptor had been paid a considerable amount of money to express the deteriorating condition of education due to the dwindling investments in university education by all levels of government; that very likely, the artist was telling us that only through commitments, monetary and personal, could our crumbling education system be resurrected. With this new referential analogue (or artificial construct), the "junk" began to metamorphose into art ... especially when the students learned that someone had been commissioned to "create" the work. I used this example with the class to underscore the point that all of us are constantly ingesting and processing new information and adding layers to our referential analogues. This is why our values and beliefs, or truths change, this is why no one agrees with another on every perception and also why there is no single immutable truth despite William Glasser's tacit claim to knowing what a "quality school" is.

"The problem, [Nils] Bohr said, was that quantum conditions ruled on the atomic scale but our instruments for measuring those conditions – our senses – ultimately worked in classical ways. That inadequacy imposed necessary limitations on what we could know ... the solution ... is to accept the different and mutually exclusive results as equally valid" (Rhodes, 1986, p. 131).

We began that first class, then, by deconstructing the perception that there is a universally just and effective school or even the Glasserian "Quality School." With that, the rocket had been fired. Whether it would ever leave the launch pad, fall into a safe, predictable orbit, or spin off on a misguided journey into the unknown, I couldn't tell. Going into the class that morning, my intentions were simple: tell the most fundamental truth I knew about "just and effective schools," then join the students for a trip that would take each of us inward rather than outward to enlarge upon "the truth."

Laura Davey (personal communication, July 9, 2011): *The opening parts of the course were philosophical introductions, studying the likes of Plato and Pirsig in order to come to an agreement about what is Truth, what is Quality and what it all means in the context of our future careers as educators, and, simply put, our futures in general. While those who have studied philosophy* **[prior]** *to this course jumped with glee at the prospect of an 'easy out,' having previously read many of the authors and texts that were chosen, others began to quake because of the stigma of philosophy as a 'difficult to understand stream' that only the 'smart ones' and 'the hippies' can really understand.* **[Pythagoras explained that a philosopher is a lover of wisdom; should not all teachers then be philosophers?]** *However, as the course evolved, students' fears were quelled through a variety of learning tactics employed by the professor – personal anecdotes, group presentations and class discussions. Some light was shed. Most began to understand the basic concepts ... several still did not. The overarching theme of the course – the concept that this course was designed for us, in order to achieve personal growth, as opposed to a hard earned (or, sometimes not so hard earned) number or letter on a group of white pages with black text scrawled across them – slowly became clear through the* *previously muddy haze that surrounded each class. While the intent of the course was genuine, sometimes the reactions were fearful. It was unknown ... we reject new ideas almost immediately if they challenge our previous beliefs. Our class initially rejected this course. I initially rejected our final exam. The only reasoning behind these rejections was personal laziness and fear. Having completed the course, I now understand why I reacted in such a way. I was afraid of going 'outside the box' because it meant doing something I may not succeed in doing.* ["All fear begins with the thought What if then continues with something disastrous" (Brahm, 2005, p. 53).] *However, that was an important lesson: failure is not a bad thing and neither is change. Allowing students to have power in the classroom and acknowledging your fallibility is a good thing. While this course cannot be fully appreciated when it is a requirement within a constructed system – ideas and theories can be introduced that truly, Truly, can change how a teacher candidate views his or her upcoming career. It might be scary at first – but, really, when is the future not?*

"If we perceive life from the perspective that all we know is a construct of consciousness, everything changes. With this shift ... we have created our perception of the world. We have given it all the meaning and value it has for us. And we are free to see it differently" (Russell, 2000, p. 93).

The following class, a small panel of students presented what they perceived to be the salient points in Bhandari's exploration of what Plato believed was and wasn't just. During the ensuing discussion, the majority of the class agreed that Cephalus's notion that "justice is doing good to friends and harm to enemies" (in Bhandari, 2000, p. 3) was flawed in a school where "equal treatment" should prevail; however, as if to reinforce the idea that consensus is rare, a few students felt that a teacher abiding by this maxim would be "justly" helping the "good students" and punishing "the bad." Not only were the terms good students and bad questioned, but several class members also questioned what "doing good" and "harm" meant. Was it harmful to punish students for their own good? Would it be good to harm recalcitrant students to improve their behavior? Clearly, the ideas of subjectivity and referential analogues were gaining supporters within the room. Some in our midst even claimed that they were actually exploring within themselves Plato's contention that justice is "an inward grace and its understanding is shown to involve a study of the inner man" (in Bhandari, 2000, p. 3).

"... when hardship strikes, we can learn not to point the finger of blame at another person, at ourselves, at an institution or even at life itself ... instead we turn our attention inward ... to look at what we ourselves have brought to the situation – beliefs, expectations, requirements, and cravings ..." (Bayda, 2002, p. 6).

Perhaps the most encouraging moment of that class occurred when one quiet back-row person raised a hand before asking:

"Wasn't it Plato who wrote about these people chained in a cave so that they could only see shadows on the wall?"

"Ah, yes ... that's the same Plato – the allegory of the cave. Anything more you recall about it?"

"Just that there were prisoners staring at the walls where

there were shadows made by people outside the cave. These guys thought the shadows were reality, then one of them escapes and discovers a whole world out there."

"Good, and what does this escapee do with his new-found reality."

"I think Plato hinted that if the guy went back into the cave and told the others they were living an illusion, they'd probably kill the guy."

"Wow ... so according to you and Plato, the cave-dwellers would prefer illusions to living in reality. Does that sound familiar?"

"Yes," came a rather urgent response from another corner of the room, "it's like people today wanting to live virtual lives instead of in reality. They would rather watch TV, play video games, go online, text messages, or read rather than live their own lives. It's the same with people using drugs ... the drugs create the shadows and we ignore our real lives."

"Plato feared the power of entertainment, the power of the senses to overthrow the mind, the power of emotion to obliterate reason. ... Plato said that the enlightened or elite had a duty to educate those bewitched by the shadows on the cave wall. ... We are chained to the flickering shadows of celebrity culture, the lies of advertising, the endless personal dramas that have become the staple of news, celebrity gossip, New Age mysticism, and pop psychology" (Hedges, 2009, p. 14).

"Good," I remarked with some astonishment at how much these people knew or how well I was teaching, "and what comment does the allegory offer about searching for 'Justice?'"

The woman responding answered as though she had been waiting a lifetime to share this thought: "That if we only look outward for Justice, or Truth, instead of within our Selves, we'll just see shadows of truth created by other people." No, it wasn't that I was teaching so well, I was simply surrounded by people who knew a great deal more than they'd ever before had reason to share. **And,** they appeared to be entertaining the option of looking inward to locate justice as Plato suggested, to find Quality as Pirsig claimed, and to discover Truth, as we shall see …

During the next class, the second panel highlighted several pivotal ideas put forth by Pirsig (1974) in *Zen and the Art of Motorcycle Maintenance*. The first was Pirsig's assertion that "Quality [is] the source and substance of everything" (p. 226).

"Imagine … shrinking one of those protons down to a billionth of its normal size … there is no space, no darkness … time doesn't exist. … In a single blinding pulse, a moment of glory much too swift and expansive for any form of words, the singularity assumes heavenly dimensions, space beyond conception" (Bryson, 2003, p. 10).

To believe Pirsig's bold contention would be to believe that there was Quality in all of the miseries, all of the pain, all of the injustices in life. The very thought of this was so incendiary that it consumed an entire two-hour class with no one defending Pirsig's assertion. At the outset of the following class, I began by pointing out that Pirsig (1974) also observed that "the reason people see Quality differently . . . is because they come to it with different sets of analogues" (p. 224). Large "Q" Quality inheres in all things, all beings, all life; it is objective, it is natural – it is the stuff of the universe – it is "space beyond comprehension" (which is an idea within our comprehension). It is through the experience of our referential analogues, then, that we conduct the process through which we label "Quality" events, experiences, or people as good or bad, just or unjust with precisely the same subjectivity and relativism that Plato described. It is on the basis of these analogues that we acknowledge one school as being "effective" and criticize another for being "ineffective." In the conventional, common-day argot, then, small "q" quality is the value that we attribute to everything that we experience through our cognition and five senses. It is the "application" of our referential analogues. It is all the descriptors that we apply to the way in which we experience being. Generally these descriptors come under one of two headings: desirable or undesirable. Of course the way in which we refer to schools, teachers, administrators, and parents would also be based upon our referential analogues and be expressed in terms such as just/unjust, effective/ineffective but these are no more absolute or valid than any other "quality" descriptors. It is on the basis of these constructs that we often predicate our behavior and interactions. In other words, as Pirsig asserts, it is a matter of mythos over logos. Put simply, we create our own personal mythologies of reality and locate ourselves in them (usually in the center). **"The mythos is a building of analogues upon analogues upon analogues. These fill the boxcars of the train of consciousness. ... The Quality is the track that directs the train"** (Pirsig, 1975, p. 137). **We live out of the mythos of society and self as though these myths are the reality or true Quality of being.**

What We Did that Day:

Instructor: "Pirsig contends that rather than living out of immediate truth or Quality, most of us live out of our own mythologies as if they were absolute truth. What might be an example of the mythology of the Self?"

Student: "If I believe that rich people are more intelligent and poor people are dull, then it's 'just' that the superior people are rewarded and that the poor people do less desirable work."

"William Howard Taft had presciently observed, 'the day is not far distant [when] the whole hemisphere will be ours in fact as by virtue of our superiority of race, it already is ours morally.' Latin Americans may not understand, the Wilson administration added, but that is because 'they are naughty children who are exercising all the privileges and rights of grown-ups' and require 'a stiff hand, an authoritative hand'" (Chomsky, 2003, p. 64).

Instructor: "Yes, that points to a personal belief system that equates material wealth with intelligence and to a social myth that is a rationale for the imbalance of wealth between individuals and between regions of our planet. Can anyone identify a myth we live out of as truth in schools?"

Student: "It is a myth when teachers tell students in the first grade that every one has an equal opportunity for success if they only work hard. It's also a myth that teachers can always tell who is smart or not and that the person with the most ability gets the highest grades. In fact grades themselves are myths – they have no more or less value than the currency of the larger society."

"I think that it is inarguable that grades do motivate some students. However, they do not motivate students to learn; rather they motivate students to produce" (Friesen, 2003, p. 9).

Instructor: "So, it may be worthwhile then for all individuals, but teachers in particular, to examine the personal myths out of which they live as well as the societal mythology … why isn't this something we commonly discuss in the schools?"

Student B: "Because once you admit that it is a myth then students start questioning what you claim to be true and also have questions about how they are graded. Also, the teacher risks having his or her own authority challenged if students think the school's power is just a collection of myths."

Socio-economic status (SES): the education status, income, and occupation of adult care-givers in the home.

Cultural capital: those tangibles and intangibles most valued by the dominant sector of a society.

Social capital: the power, position, and influence gained through social networks.

To these we may add mythological capital (K. Venema, personal communication, May, 2011) which may be defined as the power or capacity to improve one's circumstance or influence the status of others through constructs conferred by institutions or societal norms. To some extent, these may be considered the intangible aspects of cultural capital but more specifically may be named as titles, degrees, certificates, credentials, and honors.

If these four variables are key predictors of success rather than ability or intelligence, then we need to relocate the discourse on these dynamics from the university into the schools themselves. (For a more detailed discussion of SES, cultural capital, social capital, and mythological capital as variables in student performance, refer to Appendix B.)

Instructor: "Yes ... just as you appear to be questioning truths in this class putting my power at risk. Please remember this in your first year of teaching: schools are self-preserving organisms that will excise any irregularity whether in the form of a teacher or a student or an idea. The question I leave you with today, is what process or means do we rely upon to differentiate quality from Quality and myths from truth?" **"A tenth of an inch's difference, And heaven and earth are set apart." Lao Tzu**

As this class was drawing to close, one more contribution was made that seemed to encapsulate almost all that we had explored that day:

Student C Asserts: "I think that we gradually develop our social and self myths based on what is socialized and indoctrinated into us by our parents, friends, schools, churches, teachers, and media. In that sense, then, we do not act so much out of reality but we act out of what we each suppose to be real . . . what we each believe to be true or false . . . to be just or unjust. It's almost as though the lines have been scripted for us and we just act them out."

Life's but a walking shadow, a poor player,
that struts and frets his hour upon the stage,
and then is heard no more;
it is a tale told by an idiot, full of sound and fury,
signifying nothing."
William Shakespeare, *Macbeth*

Highly Impressed Instructor Agrees: "Considered in another way, Quality resides in everything that is. A table has Quality, a star, a thought, a crime, a dream, living, dying all have Quality. It is only when we apply the process of breaking off pieces of this Quality and giving these 'qualities' labels according to our referential analogues that the ubiquitous, uninterrupted Quality becomes a fragmented artificial construct."

Laura Davey (personal communication, July 9, 2011): *Students begin to realize that this course was not only about academic growth, but that the theories and concepts that were being taught were applicable – and the most beneficial when duly applied – to our everyday lives. We learned that everything we knew, believed, loved and understood was, in essence, based upon artificial constructs. I remember hearing this, and understanding it, and coming to an acceptance of the fact. It seemed logical to me. However, at the same moment, a colleague of mine had the same realization, burst into tears at the end of class, and went home for the remainder of the day. The realization that our lives are pseudo-programmed can be alarming for some. This particular colleague had come to a true moment of realization – such moments are rare, but when they occur, they can allow you a glimpse at clairvoyance.*

At the outset of the next class, however, it seemed as though the preceding days and progress were myths of my own making – everyone seemed unsettled and not very happy. My attempts at soothing the irritations which had emerged during the intervening time between classes and recapturing the clarity of the previous discussions were met with the same hostility and confusion I might have created by telling them that from this point on we would be reading and discussing Plato in the original Greek version. I was bombarded with questions and allegations that seemed to leave me pinned to the chalkboard quite uncertain if I knew what I was talking about.

"I should have been a pair of ragged claws/Scuttling across the floors of silent seas."
T. S. Eliot, *The Love Song of J. Alfred Prufrock*

"Professor," I heard one voice speak in a tone that was either inquisitive or inquisitional, "what you seem to be saying here is that Pirsig thinks that one kind of Quality exists everywhere all along and another kind we bring into existence through this artificial construction ... is that it?" Well, yes ... that is it. The voice understood. **"That which you are seeking is causing you to seek" (Huber & Shiver, 1991).** Oh my, dear class, please turn to page 317 in *Zen* ... see, there ... Pirsig (1974) writes: "Quality is the continuing stimulus which causes us to create the world in which we live." There we have the omnipresent Quality which is antecedent to all of our thoughts, indeed, to our very being and an acknowledgment that each of us brings reality into being through our being.

"The main conclusion which I have drawn from my research in the laboratory of meditation is that the ultimate nature of the universe can be described by ... the term 'Oneness' ... that the light or life emanating from the eyes of each living creature on this planet is the same light (Kezwer, 1995, p. 21). ... At the end of any scientific observation, or any perception of the world, stands the human consciousness" (p. 183).

Something was beginning take shape here. **The laboratory of the mind is where we engage in the study of our Self; out there is in here.** "Now, look back at Plato. Bhandari (2000) holds that Plato proved that "justice does not depend upon a chance, convention, or upon external forces. It is the right condition of the human soul by the very nature of man when seen in the fullness of his environment" (p. 3). Similar to Pirsig's conceptualization of Quality, justice, then, exists a priori and is discoverable only when we deconstruct convention and external forces . . . it has been there all along."

Well, we were rolling now. Getting closer to it by the moment.

"I should believe only in a God who understood how to dance" (Nietzsche, 1885/1969, p. 68).

"So," I heard a second voice which evoked even greater hopes in me, "who created this Quality – God?" Hope was displaced by desperation not only because I was uncertain of the answer but, and, I am loathe to admit, because I wondered what answer would alienate the fewest students. I had seen how the junior high students had come to view "junk" as art when they learned it had been created by a commissioned sculptor but I was uncertain how these students would view the universe if I proposed it was an unsolicited creation by the artists' artist.

... time is transition
being is participation in transition
sentience is awareness of participation
enlightenment is awareness of being

"Look," I began slowly with a different tack, "What is time?" The silence I expected. "Is it the clock on the wall? Is it the earth going around the sun?" A few hesitant "No"s.

"Well, what do those things measure?"

"Movement?" said a small voice.

"Yes! Movement ... transition. Time is transition. Without transition there is no time. Nothing to measure. Now what is 'being?'" The silence seemed greater than the stillness following the time question. "Being ... yours and mine, that of a mountain or a bird or a cloud or a virus is participation in transition. Okay?" There may have been doubters but no one in the class who had lived as long as me to think as much about the matter.

"What's the difference between us and a mountain then?" Thanks for asking.

"Sentience ... sentience is awareness of participating in being."

"So did God create Quality or not?"

"I'm not sure yet. But I do think that 'enlightenment' can get you to an understanding about that."

"And what's enlightenment?"

"I think enlightenment is awareness of being. Have you ever been profoundly aware that you are, that you exist, and you exist in a condition of being?" One nodding head out of twenty. "You have?"

"Yeah ... it was scary"

"Why scary?"

"Because I also thought about not being and realized how fragile life is."

"Yeah, me too, but did you also understand that through your awareness, through your thoughts and being that you were bringing all of what you sensed and understood into existence?"

"Are you saying we're God?

"I'm saying that whatever brought Quality into being also brought you into being and that you create the universe through that being. I want to be careful here, but I think that I'm also saying that the absolute truth, the Quality of that universe and Plato's 'justice' lies still within you ... and within me." **... I bring the Universe into being as it brings me into being.**

"I wanna go home."

"To think, I hope."

"No, to quit thinking ... this is giving me a headache." **"... just hang in there and float lightly in the sea of confusion ... it signals that something new and interesting is underway" (Gregson & Efran, 2002, p. 63).**

"That's up to you ... actually everything is up to you." ... **"I alone am the honored one." (Traditional Zen Commentary)**

Laura Davey (personal communication, July 9, 2011): *As the course progressed, conversational language changed drastically outside the university classroom. At least once, in almost every conversation held with my colleagues, someone would say "Yes, but that is your own referential analogue" or "that may be Your Truth, but it is not Mine." We were given a new vocabulary to speak to one another with – a vocabulary that allowed for debate, discussion and, at times, discord.*

Despite the forward-backward dance that first group of students was improvising, I felt as though some deconstruction of "The Mythos" was beginning, and the more I thought about it, the more I realized that this halting tempo was exactly correct for that time and that place and those individuals – to dash toward some misbegotten notion of truth and enlightenment would be to ignore the process necessary for thoughtful inquiry, and it would also put individuals in jeopardy when they endeavored to discard the myths that had guided them for their lifetimes. That students were starting to glimpse the notion that so much of what schools are is abstract and not immutable truth was, perhaps, enough. For them to suspect that marks, assessments, grade levels, codes of behavior, proper conduct, obedience, attitude, values ... all these elements considered cornerstones of schooling and aspects of the school were mere intellectual constructs rather than Quality truths, was a great deal of information and understanding. **These are the mythologies of the institution and the myths of the self brought into conflict with the Truth of the Self.** I endeavored to appreciate and respect the challenge students would face in letting go of these notions which had been so deeply ingrained in all of us ... so important to many of us. To understand them as artificial constructs or myths was difficult if not dangerous for those of us who had built our self-concepts upon these ideas and drew upon them for our esteem – this was a maxim I endeavored to embrace as a guide for all sections of this course.

Before you attempt the extraordinary, you must accomplish the ordinary.

Laura Davey (personal communication, July 9, 2011): *The course lent itself to being a guide in discovering our own senses of self – who we are and what we believe and it helped us to examine how our beliefs are going to affect our teaching and our students. As teachers, we learned, we can only teach our Truth, as WE know it, to our students. We cannot expect our students to adopt our Truth – because it would be unjust and ineffective. It would continue to perpetuate a cycle of students who are not adept at critical thinking and who blindly follow tradition. Just as we were being enlightened about the fallibility of "the grade" and the sheer audacity as the attempt to "grade" one's work, Professor Bergsgaard allowed us the opportunity to do away with this traditional approach. Writing this now, I appreciate it; however, at the time I had several frustrations. My first reaction, as I analyze it now, was sourced out of fear. It was an unknown format for a class and I felt, at times, that it was an 'easy way out' for the professor. No papers to mark, no final exams to grade. At the same time, however, I was excited: no memorization of authors and their theories, no notes on who said what about which topic. No pointless exam about specific material I will likely forget about in three months. Instead, we were given the opportunity to discuss the concepts that we had learned, rather than memorize details and facts. We were being permitted to explore the [deeper] layers of Bloom's Taxonomy, rather than regurgitating facts about specific authors.*

In many regards, the way the course was playing out reminded me of the regrets I still harbored over discussing nihilism many years earlier with a class of grade 10 students. I could see in virtually every face in that high school classroom that they didn't necessarily want confirmation of their suspicions that life had no meaning; the part about shaping essence out of existence never got across and I left them standing on the precipice. I had resolved, however, that after initiating the "deconstruction" of the just and effective school, my role in the class would be no different from the student – to quest for the most fundamental form of Truth.

"The quotations of philosophers, literati, and theorists reflect the thoughts of people whose ideas are based on their constructs and referential analogues, no less than are mine. In searching for justice and authenticity in schools, I am forced to engage in a process of deconstructing the myths on which schools are built. Moreover, I require myself to engage in a process of deconstructing the myths on which beliefs I have accepted for the better part of twenty-six years are built. This is a process that requires great personal effort and reflection. It is a process that I feel is flawed and incomplete, but honest ... it is an attempt to look inward, close my eyes and follow the Truth, Quality or Stimulus that resides within the cells of my humanity" (Friesen, 2003, p. 42).

Student A to Instructor at the beginning of the next class: "I'm with the group that's presenting today on Russell's chapter [*From Science to God*]. Would it be okay if we just began without you doing a lot of talking first?"

Instructor: "As we've said, my truth is no more important than yours; it might be a good idea if I began to recede into the class as just one of the group – you people won't take advantage of me will you? It's a bit frightening to give up control like this ..."

Student A: "This is a bit frightening for all of us – it isn't your usual education course."

Instructor: "No ... I don't know whether to apologize or boast."

Student A to Class: "Michel Foucault said the following in an interview: 'My role ... is to show people that they are much freer than they feel.' Can anyone in here see how that relates to this observation from Russell?" (2000):

"Everything we know, perceive, and imagine, every color, sound, sensation, thought, and feeling is a form the consciousness has taken on. As far as this world is concerned, everything is structured in consciousness. ... Kant argued that this was even true of space and time" (p. 56).

If we in that room were actually bringing time into existence, we seemed to have made it stand still. It was possibly the longest pause in a discussion I had ever witnessed, but our student would not yield.

"... every datum used by science in formulating its supposedly objective worldview comes in through the human senses. Every attempt at making an impartial objective observation is foiled at the outset and becomes, instead, a subject of our personal attention. The human observer cannot be left out of the reckoning or be reduced to insignificance, because he or she is the very means by which science is prosecuted ... within the emotion-filled, perception-charged, *conscious* environment of the human mind" (Darling, 1996, p. 127).

Finally, an intrepid student who had not said anything to that point in the course:

"I think what Russell is saying is that whether we're a human being or a dolphin, we all bring the universe into being through our awareness of it. A dolphin uses sonar. I use five senses and my mind. Either way, that understanding of reality is an understanding of Pirsig's Quality. What that means, though, is that we all have a legitimate claim to the truth of our Selves. It's when we start adding ideas and opinions or mistake quality for Quality that we get confused but as Foucault said, we are free to make choices about how we think."

"To the question 'what must I do to free myself?' Zen replies: 'There is nothing you need do since you have never been enslaved and since there is nothing in reality from which you can free yourself'" (Benoit, 1990, p. 4). In effect, the only limits on our freedom are those created in and by our own minds.

Student A: "Excellent ... Russell believes that we bring the universe into being through our consciousness, Pirsig claims that our consciousness is Quality, and Plato tells us to check in with that pure consciousness for truth. And you're saying Foucault's assertion is that the limits on what we think are self-imposed. What about feelings? Are we free to choose how we feel?"

Student C: "I had this conversation with my partner. He said I made him mad and I told him that my words were just that ... sounds ... Big Q Quality ... whatever he felt in response to what I said, was what he chose to feel."

Student A: "So you're saying that we can choose to feel angry or not."

Student C: "I'm saying the same thing Foucault is saying, that we have a lot more freedom to choose how we think and feel than we suspect. It's liberating to realize I don't have to get mad at someone if I don't want to but it's also frustrating because sometimes I like feeling mad."

Instructor: "Yes, we do all like living out of our little dramas as though they are being played out across a universal stage. Let me ask though, based upon Russell, Pirsig, and Foucault, where is the only place in the universe that these dramas are actually happening?"

Student A (who looks straight at the Instructor): "In my own mind ... I bring it into being."

***

To the reader: Thanks for your patience, persistence, and curiosity if you are still with us. We can take a bit of a break here since this was a transition point in the course and you may need one as I typically do. Although it is by no means predictable nor essential, at this point in the course we have usually come to agree that for Quality, Absolute Truth, Justice, or Freedom, one must look inward. We also usually concur that each of us is entitled to the truth that we discover during this inward search and that students and children have just as much of a claim to truth as do teachers and other adults. This is usually quite a fearsome epiphany, since individuals in our course begin to imagine their own classrooms where everyone has a valid claim to reality and I am at a point where I know that the students in that room are beginning to question my authority, my claim to quality as Quality, and, as much as anything, my right to confer upon them a grade as a quality judgment on the Quality of their thoughts. It is with this uncertainty that we take the class forward into a more specific examination of societal mythologies all the while holding tightly to our emerging recognition that we are all simultaneously and individually bringing reality into being through our being … every second we are in the classroom or outside of it.

With the next panel, that search began on several levels.

**"If you have come here to help me,
You are wasting your time.
But if you have come here because your liberation is bound up with mine, then let us work together."
(Lilla Watson, Brisbane-based Aboriginal educator and activist)**

If a teacher does not truly feel hope for the future of humankind, how may that teacher inspire hope in students? More disconcerting yet is the teacher who does not know what he or she thinks or feels.

Two critical ideas emerged from the third panel's presentation on Freire's (1970) *Pedagogy of the Oppressed*. From the outset, the students were emphatic in their agreement with Freire that the oppressors, whether bourgeois university professors or "typical" teachers in the schools, had to abandon their misplaced intentions to impose their values, beliefs, and behaviors upon the oppressed whether they be the poor and disenfranchised or students in any educational institution. The second point stressed by the panel was the necessity for Freire's (1970) "praxis" or shared "reflection and action" (p. 33) between the oppressor and oppressed to create the dialectic necessary for "change upon the world in order to transform it" (p. 33). As the group reported, it was Freire's (1970) belief that "the oppressed must confront reality critically, simultaneously objectifying and acting upon that reality. A mere perception of reality not followed by this critical intervention will not lead to a transformation ... precisely because it was not a true perception" (p. 34).

Student K: "I agree with Freire that we need to think about our actions before and after we perform them. I also agree that instead of using a middle-class white perspective on change, or the attitude of 'be more like me and you too shall succeed,' we need to engage in this praxis together without expecting a particular outcome. That's why I don't like the term reflection – it suggests other people should just accept and mirror back the ideas of the oppressor. Since we're doing more than just reflecting and acting, why not just call the process 'refraction.' Refraction is the bending or changing of a wave, which is what we do when we interact with events and ideas. It's also a combination of the words: reflection and action."

Instructor: I think you just refracted something wonderful into existence, Kris.

"It may strike us as odd that the idea of gain is a relatively modern one, we are schooled to believe that man is essentially an acquisitive creature and that left to himself he will behave ... as any businessman would. The profit motive, we are constantly being told, is as old as man himself. But it is not. The profit motive as we know it is only as old as 'modern man.' Even today the notion of gain for gain's sake is foreign to a large portion of the world's population, and it has been conspicuous by its absence over most of recorded history" (Heilbroner, 1953, p. 24).

The fuse had been lit. It seemed that Freire (1970), too, was saying that much of education, traditional pedagogy, and our "reality," is based upon myths, quality, or subjective perception. When he writes that transformation occurs "through the expulsion of the myths created and developed in the old order, which like specters haunt the new structure" (p. 37), he appears to be affirming my contention that much of what we accept as truths in schooling are merely constructs and Pirsig's assertion that, left unexamined, personal and cultural myths will predict "logic" rather than the inverse. This radical vision of education, of being, seemed to be getting the attention of the students.

Along with insight, however, there was also emerging an indignation bordering on anger that this perception had never been offered to them in their years of schooling, in their years of university education.

"The real purpose of these richly endowed [Ivy League] schools is to perpetuate their own. They do this even as they pretend to embrace the ideology of the common man, trumpet diversity on campus and pose as a meritocracy. ... at the elite institutions, those on the inside are told they are there because they are better than others. Most believe it. They see their money and their access to power as a natural extension of their talents and abilities, rather than the result of a system that favors the privileged. ... The elites vacation together, ski at the same Swiss resorts, and know the names of the same restaurants in New York and Paris ... they speak an intimidating language of privilege, complete with references to minutiae and traditions only the elite understand. They have obtained a confidence those on the outside often struggle to duplicate. And the elite, while they may not say so in public, disdain those who lack their polish and connections" (Hedges, 2009, p. 98-100).

If the philosophical and pedagogical architecture of education was based upon artificial constructs, why had they not been told? Why had they not seen it? Shouldn't a revelation this basic and profound be reported on CNN or tweeted on Twitter? Was the system so efficient in selling this illusion that no one, not students, not teachers, not principals, saw through it? The fuse had been lit and I was sitting on the powder keg toward which it burned.

"... the biggest influence on educational attainment, how well a child performs in school and later in higher education, is family background. ... Children do better if their parents have higher incomes and more education themselves, and they do better if they come from homes where they have a place to study, where there are reference books and newspapers, and where education is valued. Parental involvement in children's education is even more important" (Wilkinson & Pickett, 2009, p. 103).

The next class began with me returning a set of papers which I had corrected and graded. As usual, I gave the students a bit of time to look over my comments and the grades which I had assigned.

"Professor," from somewhere came an agitated voice followed by an arm in the air which I traced to a face, "What are all these artificial constructs doing on my paper? And you've got a 'B+' on here, too ... What's that supposed to mean? To me this may have been an 'A' paper or a 'C' ... Why is it that your truth counts for more?" The keg had exploded and, in that instant, the class became a laboratory studying itself ... we became a class studying ourselves.

Laura Davey (personal communication, July 9, 2011): *Trying to sum up the experiences I had in Just and Effective Schools brought to mind the comedy sketch of Colin Mochrie and Brad Sherwood when they perform in front of an audience, blindfolded and barefoot, with 300 live mouse traps on the stage. The experience is stressful and painful for the performers, not only when a live trap snatches a pinkie toe, but because of* *the fear of the impending traps. At the end of the routine, there appears to be a sense of satisfaction from the performers, knowing that they had just experienced truly 'living in the moment,' even though the experience, at the time, is terrifying. Our course was quite similar. Throughout, there were moments of fear and pain; however, at the end of the course we can reflect on our experiences and know that we have come out successful.*

"Well, my 'truth' counts for more because I'm the teacher. That's probably what your teachers told you and, most likely, that's what you're going to fall back on some day."

"Why is the teacher's truth the only truth?"

"What would happen if everyone's truth were equal? Can you imagine a classroom where students' views were given the same credibility and respect as the teachers? That would be like the praxis Freire was talking about, wouldn't it? What if the oppressed were suddenly as empowered as the oppressors? We don't know what would happen when the 'oppressors meet the oppressed.' It could be total chaos. It certainly wouldn't be what most people currently expect of schools in terms of justness and effectiveness, would it"

"Well, why are we doing all this talking about grades as artificial constructs and the relativity of justness and effectiveness but you apply your constructs and subjectivity to our work?"

"Because I am old and wise, I have more education, and my referential analogues are more well developed than yours. Or, to paraphrase a colleague, I have more 'mythological capital' than you (K. Venema, personal communication, May, 2011)." Whether the students laughed or not, this was institutional apocrypha and they knew it; the contradiction between what we were saying in class and doing in class had become obvious as I had thought it might. What I didn't know was how to resolve it. "Look, you peeps (a collective pronoun one class had suggested I employ rather than the gender-bound 'guys' I used but they didn't like), you're right. I've got to think about this, though; you've got to think about it, okay? Now we've got another panel waiting to get up here," I said, conspicuously buying time.

"According to Carolyn Shrewsbury (1987), 'critical thinking is not an abstracted analysis but a reflective process firmly grounded in the experiences of the everyday'" (p. 7) concluded the first panelist; not only had this student offered up a meaningful insight into feminist pedagogy, she also offered up the answer I had been struggling to find while concurrently trying to listen to her presentation.

I interjected, "In telling us that we must reflect – or refract – as we act to discover truths, she is advising us similarly to whom?"

"Freire, with praxis; reflection in action – or Kris's 'refraction,'" responded someone sounding rather pleased.

"Yes, Freire. Freire advocated a reflective process, as well – much the same as Plato directing us inward for Justice. Actually, I'm going to beg the panel's indulgence and go off on a bit of a tangent here; maybe it will give more meaning to this reflection and looking at 'truth' in the classroom.

A classroom, in particular lends itself to being described as "... the unimpeded inter-diffusion of all particulars" (Suzuki, in Humphreys, 1985, p. 58).

"Let's suppose you're the teacher in a grade-8 language arts class, a student unexpectedly gets out of his seat, walks to the door and attempts to leave the room. You ask, 'Where do you think you're going?' With an angry tone, the student responds, 'I'm leaving.' You shoot back with, 'You're not going anywhere until you get permission. Now get back in here and sit down!' The student slams the door as he leaves the room; you race after him and shout, 'I'd like to see you after school.' When you catch up to the student, you see a look of distress on his face and in a sympathetic tone inquire whether there is a problem. More out of discomfort than anger, the student tersely explains, 'I'm sick, gotta go to the washroom.' At this point your fear and uncertainty give way to concern and you ask if there is anything you might be able to do.

"Now, when he gets up to leave, you interpret the student's behavior as a threat as soon as that behavior is inconsistent with the rules or system of 'justness' developed for the class. This is threatening to you as your imagination rapidly conjures up countless possibilities: Are you losing your power? Your control of the classroom? If this student challenges your authority, the other students might all get up and leave. What if the principal walks by? You don't believe you deserve this disrespect. You must regain control. These ideas cause you to perceive the behavior as a threat to your security and well-being.

Fear is the unacknowledged backdrop in most teachers' lives.

"First we need to see that we are all afraid. Our basic fear is of death, and this fear is the basis of all other fears. Our fear of our own annihilation leads to useless behaviors, including the effort to protect our self-image, or ego. Out of that need to protect comes anger. Out of anger comes conflict. And conflict destroys our relationships with others" (Beck, 1993, p. 97).

Although they are only ideas and not the reality of the event, you react to them with fear that you may lose control, respect, and your job because of one 'bad' kid. It is fear that provokes you to demand the student's obedience. When he refuses to comply and leaves the room, a feeling of powerlessness arises. As you go after the child, ideas occur in your mind according to your construct of justice, your desire to regain control, and your indignation over the trouble being caused for you. These ideas sustain or redouble your fear and it is out of anger, generated entirely by illusions, that you interact with the child and command him to stop. However, as soon as you see the look of distress on the student's face, the cycle of thought-emotion is broken and the illusions from which you acted dissipate. Now, the perception of distress provokes the idea that something is amiss with the child and you realize that your reactions may have been inappropriate. It occurs to you to ask about the child's welfare to acquire the information you need to quiet the growing sense of guilt and concern you have about the consequences for the student's inappropriate behavior. Upon hearing the student's reason for leaving the room, it becomes clear in an instant that his disregard for the rules likely resulted from his fear of being embarrassed by having to explain to his classmates the source of urgency in his departure. Putting yourself in the student's position, you now feel sympathy and compassion. Either of these emotions would be sufficient to prompt you to offer assistance to the student.

"What is most remarkable in all of this is that the strongest, most stressful feelings for you were not based on the simple reality of one human being leaving a room, but issued out of ideas based upon assumptions and illusions about justice and effectiveness that provoked emotion which provoked a further acceleration of the process through which we develop constructs … not pure reality, but constructs or referential analogues as

Pirsig might term them. Additionally, acting out of this cycle, it was impossible for you to respond appropriately to the needs of the student. (For a more detailed description of the reciprocal interplay between thoughts and feelings as well as the Self Observing, please refer to Appendix A.)

"Just let things happen as they do. Let all images and thoughts and sensations arise and pass away without being bothered, without reacting, without judging, without clinging. ... Keep the mind sharply aware, moment to moment of what is happening ... with a balanced and relaxed mind" (Goldstein, 1976, p. 28).

"Had you, as the teacher, practiced reflection in action, you more likely would have recognized that you were feeling threatened as well as fearful and, rather than acting out of those emotions, would have responded out of a more informed sensibility so that this event would have unfolded in a less stressful way for you, and in a more caring and compassionate way toward the student and the rest of the class. If through reflection upon previous experience, you had developed for yourself the strategy of letting the fear and anger pass or responded to the student's rising from the chair with the question, 'Is there anything I can do to help you?' the subsequent series of events would have been quite unlike the sequence recounted above."

"By surfing the waves of thought and emotion, you ride them safely back to shore and allow them to ebb away of their own accord" (Gregson & Efran, 2002, p. 97).

"But wouldn't Pirsig say that there is Quality in either event?"

"Yes," I agreed, "there is the Quality that arises out of 'beingness' in either event. But part of 'being' as human is our ability to imagine or create beyond what is pure reality using our imaginations and referential analogues. The key here is to recognize what we each uniquely and individually are creating and to realize the relativity of that truth … to recognize the difference between constructed reality and pure reality, between quality and Quality. Now, we have one more panelist to go."

"Well, there's only five more minutes of class," the remaining panelist pointed out.

"We do not see things as they are but as the brain interprets them for us (Barbour, 1999, p. 28) … time does not exist. All that exists are things that change" (p. 137).

"Sorry … I stole your time; in five minutes, what occurs to you as the most important thing that Shrewsbury is saying?"

"Well, the need for reflecting; the same as Freire. But she also writes about men in power having created schools in which there is top-down authority, 'the morality of rights is dominant' and those rights are decided by the authorities, and schools value individualism and competition. Shrewsbury (1987) wouldn't see this as a just and effective school; her model seems more like something Freire would agree with. Here's a quote:

> The vision includes a participatory, demo-
> cratic process in which at least some of the
> power is shared. Learners develop indepen-
> dence. The classroom becomes a model of
> ways for people to work together to
> accomplish mutual or shared goals, and to
> help each other reach individual goals (p. 7)
> ... [it is] actively engaged with others in a
> struggle to get beyond our sexism and
> racism and classism and homophobia and
> other destructive hatreds and to work
> together to enhance our knowledge ... with
> movements for social change. (p. 6)

If you think of sexism, racism, classism, and homophobia as constructs, then what Shrewsbury is saying is what Professor was telling us about deconstructing illusions like this through reflection and discovering basic reality."

"I said that? Well that's pretty profound for me."

"Yeah, but how do we learn this reflection? You haven't told us. ... Neither has Freire or any of the others. I can't just start deconstructing my myths or societal myths without some kind of map to follow!"

"How do you think we learn it? Where do you think the treasure map is buried? Maybe next class when our colleagues present to us on bell hooks."

If the social capital, cultural capital, mythological capital, and socio-economic status of a student's family are the most reliable predictors of success (or failure in schools), then the

assertion that schools are meritocratic is a myth at best and a deception at worst – it is a myth which allows the school to blame the child for the child's failure. We must relocate the discourse on capital into the schools with the students.

I have seen, and occasionally written, course outlines in which professors detail down to the hour on a specific date what will happen during the term. In the instance of this course – whether in 2001 or 2013 – I couldn't have said with any certainty where we would be after the first twenty minutes of the first day. I knew that I had chosen carefully the readings we would examine and that they were sequenced to coincide with my efforts to deconstruct the perception that there was a universally accepted understanding of what a just and effective school is. However, based upon the work I had been doing with Contemplative Practice, I also sensed that, at some juncture, all of us in the classroom were going to have to turn inward to examine not only our own dearly held opinions about just and effective but also the fact that these opinions were merely artificial constructs.

"Contemplation in Merton's view involves a reconnecting with the fundamental unity of life ... the Source. The Christian contemplative Steindl-Rast has simply called this source 'home.' Steindle-Rast states, 'this longing for belonging, this homing instinct of the heart, is the path within every path.' Contemplation, then can be viewed as the way to be 'at home'" (Miller, 1994, p. 3).

I also knew that once students began deconstructing personal myths, they would then apply that same powerful critique to larger mythologies including those which provided the infrastructure of the academy to which our class belonged.

What I didn't know was how I could direct students who had been taught for a lifetime to seek answers from the external environment to begin an examination of their own interiors and what form that process of examination would take. By this point in the course, however, it appeared that most of the students were anxious to explore the idea of reflection or Self-Observation and the work of bell hooks was invaluable in providing a direction. What the reader may see in the coming passages, then, is a convergence of the earlier part of the course where we examine the journey inward to locate the truth of our selves, with the next part of the course in which we apply that process for separating myth from truth, and quality from Quality, to the external environment. Said another way, we look at our world, our schools, our lives with confidence in our ability to discern absolute truth from constructs and the courage to act mindfully out of that restored clarity.

"My energy shifted. ... I am now at one with the universe. I have blended into the eternal flow and am beyond returning to this plane of life – yet I remain tethered here" (Bolte-Taylor, 2006, p. 68).

The panel of students which discussed the excerpt from *Teaching to Transgress* (hooks, 1994) seemed to have sensed the flow toward inner examination; they skillfully built upon Plato's truth within, Freire's concepts of praxis, and Shrewsbury's thinking on reflection, then began to talk about the necessity for teachers to know themselves and who it was they were taking into the classroom. A crucial nexus between all of the ideas we had been exploring was written by hooks (1994) and quoted by a panelist:

> Progressive, holistic education, 'engaged pedagogy' is more demanding than conventional critical or feminist pedagogy. For unlike these two teaching practices, it emphasizes well-being. That means that teachers must be actively committed to a process of self-actualization that promotes their own well-being if they are to teach in a manner that empowers students. (p. 15)

What hooks appears to be saying in the quotation is that personal development is a necessary antecedent to professional development. My question, my quest, the students' question, their quest was, How do we become "self-actualized" in order to develop personally and professionally? After the panel presentation, I read the quote again to the class, then suggested, "This seems to take us back to a question from the last class: 'How do we, as educators, learn to reflect inwardly?' When you have your own classroom how will you teach yourselves to observe your inner selves ... to watch yourselves constructing illusions out of reality in the midst of a class?"

"You must know that it is no easy thing for a principle to become a man's [or woman's] own, unless each day [s]he maintain it and hear it maintained, as well as work it out in life" (Epictetus in Humphreys, 1985, p. 49).

"We go home and think about our teaching ..."

"You go home and think about it how? Worry about it? Think about how you're going to get things to go your way in the classroom?"

"No, just what went well and what didn't."

"According to whom? To you? To a student? How are you going to assess that?"

"You don't have to measure it; you just know it."

"Okay, but what mechanism or process are you going to have in place so that you do this regularly? This was a concern expressed in the previous class. And please don't forget that perception, then feeling, often precedes thought. How are you going to routinely watch your perceptions?"

"Keep a journal?"

"Good … that's good. How many of you have ever started a journal? Okay, most of us. How many of you still keep one? Okay, two of us. But why did so many of us stop? For me it was because it was impossible to capture on paper the complexities of a moment, let alone a day, and it didn't really prepare me to think or behave with different feelings or thoughts the next day. What else could give us the structure or motivation to practice to reflect, to Self-Observe, to watch our thoughts and feelings?"

"How about talking with someone every night?"

"That can work especially if that person helps us to deconstruct the illusions we've built, but it still doesn't train us to 'watch in the moment.' What if I told you that bell hooks has an interest in Zen Buddhism and you put that idea together with the title of Pirsig's book … what does that give us?"

"Meditation ..."

"Okay ... meditation to do what?"

"To stop your thinking."

"Some people probably do meditate with the idea of stopping their thoughts. But there is another form of meditation that involves watching your thoughts and noticing your feelings. Most often, we think that we are in control of our thoughts and our feelings. That's one reason we feel secure going into a classroom thinking our notion of just and effective is the correct one. But when you locate yourself in a quiet place, get situated in a meditative position, and try to observe your thoughts, you'll likely be amazed not by the control you have but how ideas, images, and words constantly arise and fall away in your mind like a movie or tape recorder playing. You can see how some thoughts just naturally disappear and others you latch on to and use to construct more grandiose and elaborate ideas. When you spend more time with this, you begin to see how these ideas evoke emotions which then charge or fuel the ideas much the same as the teacher in the class where the student walked out. If you become very practiced in this study, you can take it forward into your daily life, watch how you construct, then notice how your constructions cause emotions and how those emotions, in turn, cause more construction. With this 'watching' you can observe yourself becoming angry, afraid, happy, excited. It's precisely what I was talking about in the instance of a student dashing from the classroom without permission. You then are getting to know your Self in a way that allows you to recognize what might frighten you or make you angry and how to deal with those feelings as you watch them rise and fall away. It doesn't mean you won't feel anger or fear, but you begin to silently name each, watch it fall away, and watch that you aren't acting out of fear." (A reminder: for a more detailed description of the Self Observing the interplay between thought-feeling please refer to Appendix A.)

"We can meditate and attain realization in our daily work, in contact with people, in trying to understand ... them. Truth or reality is everywhere. If we have the capacity to realize it, it is with us everywhere and all the time" (Thien-An, 1975, p. 38).

"So are you saying we'll stop thinking and feeling?"

"Meditation is not evasion; it is a serene encounter with reality. ... The sadness or anxiety, hatred or passion, under the gaze of concentration and meditation reveals its own nature – a revelation that leads naturally to healing and emancipation" (Nhat Hanh, 1975, p. 60-61).

"No ... never; being as humans predicts that our nature is to think and feel. Artificial constructs are invaluable to us. They allow us to imagine, to create, to have empathy as well as to worry, anticipate, and construct illusions. I don't want you to drive a car without some regard for the rules of the road and I don't expect to steal your laptop with impunity simply because the law against it is a construct. What meditation gives us is a structure to practice watching our Selves feel and think so that we develop awareness between constructed reality and artificial reality, between quality and Quality. But it's not something you do once then do naturally forever. You do have to practice it."

"The social structure we live in continually reinforces the ego through competition and fear ... meditation lets us witness the striving of the ego ... and very gradually we begin to see that our fundamental identity is not the thoughts that form our ego structure but the clear awareness that is witnessing the arising and falling of all

these thoughts. This basic insight is the beginning of liberation and compassion" (Miller, 1994, p. 7).

"How does that allow you to become a more just or more effective teacher?"

"Because you learn to see what is real and what is artificial" ...

"We meditate to find, to recover, to come back to something of ourselves we once dimly and unknowingly had and have lost without knowing what it was or where or when we lost it" (LeShan, 1974, p. 3).

... in the classroom scenario we discussed, you understand that pure reality or Quality was the student getting out of a chair and leaving a room; our feelings were Quality, as well, but most of the thoughts were constructs emanating out of our unique referential analogues and once we recognize that, we learn to choose how we act out of them. We understand that our thoughts are ephemeral and not absolute truths – we see, also, that others act out of constructs based upon their referential analogues as though they were absolute truth. We bring this process of deconstructing myths into the larger environment. We deconstruct television commercials, blogs, political slogans, religious rhetoric, and everything we read anywhere. That doesn't mean we then abandon the myths we sort from Quality, but that we begin to interact with them as constructs rather than absolute, inviolable truths of the universe which we must accept. Once we have begun this work in our minds, we share the process with students who act blindly out of personal or societal myths. This we do carefully with the understanding that they, too, must seek inward for their truth at a pace that is healthy for each.

"When we introspect, we find that every thought that occurs affects all the thoughts that follow" (Sekida, 1985, p. 121).

Once the Self observes the mind thinking and feeling, thinking and feeling, all future thoughts and feelings are informed by the Self's awareness of this reciprocal process. In other words, when we become observers of our own thoughts and feelings, the universe and events in it have been changed forever.

Student: "I sort of get this, but we're all still a little confused. Don't you have another story to give as an example."

Instructor: "I appreciate your patience and your interest; actually I can give you a story. I was working in the inner city with children deemed to be gifted and I was given an office in one school where I could do administrative work. In that school a teacher told me that she had a very challenging student who was very bright, very sensitive, very angry, and very close to spending his life in prison; she asked if I would meet with him. On the appointed day, a lad of about fourteen came into the office, barely glanced at me before looking around the office then fixing his glare on the floor between us. During the course of a largely desultory and dispiriting conversation, he looked up once more at the walls and was inspired to remark, 'Your walls look like xxxx. In fact your whole office looks like xxxx.' Trying to float above the insult I suggested he might have to become accustomed to looking at xxxxxx walls if it truly was his life's mission to become a criminal. He then shot an angry scowl my way before I asked him, 'What do you like doing besides hanging out with your friends?'

'Like being with my girlfriend. Like partying. Like stealin' rides.'

'Okay, can you now try to imagine how much time you'll be spending with your girlfriend in the detention center? Think they do a lot of partying in prison? Lotta car stealing? You're living out of the myth that you're the toughest guy on the streets and that you'll use prison as a badge of courage. Why don't you go away, think about living in this xxxxxx office for twenty years without any of the things you enjoy ... try that illusion on.'

"This was a simple matter of inviting the young man to examine the constructs or myths out of which he lived or which had been imposed upon him. That's the great part of recognizing our freedom to imagine consequences. Once we project possible scenarios on the basis of what we imagine or others help us to imagine, we can experience the possible rewards and consequences before we endeavor to make either a reality. I forgot about this kid until about a month later when he slouched into my office and, without a word, tossed a remarkable drawing on my desk. I told him it was nice and asked if I could keep it. I was shocked when he said that the drawing wasn't for me to keep; rather, it was a rough template of the mural he would paint on my walls if I wanted. I doubted that the school, a 'self' preserving institution, would allow mural painting, but in later talking with the principal we agreed that, in this instance, the policy allowing only unionized employees to paint walls could be ignored. Another myth refracted. The art teacher was able to find enough money in his budget for supplies to buy paint and brushes, and the classroom teacher adjusted her constructs on attendance to allow the boy to spend two classes a week in my office. Now it took months for this to unfold, but each day that this young man worked, the jagged edges seemed to round off of his persona. Other teachers and students would stop by to admire the work he was doing as he painted. In short, his personal mythology was changing. He began to understand that he could make choices that resulted in him feeling connected in more positive ways than when he and his peers were stealing cars. He began to see that the myth that he had constructed about him Self as an outsider who used fear and anger to shield himself was not the way he had to be in the world."

"[spiritually gifted] individuals ... illustrate the ability to reach beyond the self and to connect with the divine. Each is

dedicated to living a courageous life of self-reflection and transformation. Daily, they strive to live in accordance with an inner barometer, which requires listening to and embracing the complex nature of their intellectual, emotional, physical, social, and spiritual selves. No longer feeling compelled to please others, they consciously choose to be open and accepting of whatever comes their way. Instead of submitting to an internalized inner authority or controlling voice, their daily goal is to simply be who they are called from within to be ... the daily war within – to quiet old tapes of self-demands and judgments, and to follow inner guidance and an intuitive way of knowing – has grown easier over many months and years" (Gatto-Walden, 2009, p. 218).

It was no different than the time I invited a university student to strive for a B+ to unburden himself of the myth that he was an A person; or the time I told the ninth grade class-clown that he didn't have to spend the year entertaining us – one could almost watch the relief these young people felt when the weight of the mythology was lifted and they were free to become other than what they believed they were – they could always go back, but now there was a choice – just as Foucault suggested. In the case of the artist, he also began to realize that biased views held toward him because of his ethnicity, past behavior, and family history were not absolute truth – he began to understand that it was possible for him to be respected by other people he believed had always excluded him. The key point in this, though, is that I would not have thought to share the process of deconstruction with him, had I not embarked upon that journey my Self. We don't conduct this search for truth out of self-interest alone, but for the well-being of others. Does that help?"

Student: "It does if it was a true story."

Instructor: "It's a truthful description of how I brought the experience into being. The views of anyone else may differ but may be just as true. Let's take a more immediate example we've touched on in this class before. If you see that grades are really just abstract constructs, you work with them in a different way with students. In many cases, the artificiality becomes so evident that you want to abandon grades altogether because you see that the construct is what students strive for; not for the joy in learning or creating but to get grades ... like getting a salary. You also see what a deleterious effect getting bad grades can have on children because they perceive grades as true indicators of their personal worth and integrate that assessment into their personal mythologies."

"The objective mechanisms which enable the ruling classes to keep the monopoly of the most prestigious education establishments, while continually appearing at least to put the chance of possessing that monopoly into the hands of every generation, are concealed beneath the cloak of a perfectly democratic method of selection which takes into account only merit and talent" (Bourdieu, 2000, p. 61).

... marking is as much an emotional experience as an intellectual exercise ... it divides as much as it connects. One of the greatest gifts we may give to students is a sense of rightful belonging ... belonging in our class, our community,

our universe. Too often, grades create impediments to belonging.

"Well, if that's true, why are you giving us grades in here? That last mark you gave me didn't do much for my mythology."

"As I reflect on my own education, I have come to realize how entrenched the idea is that my worth can be measured by my grades. I realize how blindly I have accepted the construct that good grades make me a good student, a good daughter, and a good person. The process of becoming aware of the artifice of this construct and working to deconstruct it is one that is fraught with difficulty and questioning. I am forced to ask myself where I find my worth, if not in the opinions of my teachers" (Friesen, 2003, p. 10).

At this juncture in the course, it was distressingly apparent to everyone that while we were discussing the disturbing effects of marks and mythos in the school system, we were replicating the very same effects in our classroom. The only difference was that the students in our room now understood the dynamics and were more than anxious to identify and confront them. To describe those dynamics and tensions of the closing days from a student's perspective, I wish to step aside and allow James Tyson, a member of the original Just and Effective class to share his thoughts and feelings:

It was while writing the "White Pines" paper (for the Just and Effective Schools course) that I realized that my innate need to learn was never met during my years of schooling. As soon as I recognized this I quickly made the connection that there was a contradiction in the Just and Effective Schools course between what we were learning and how we were being evaluated by the professor. I reasoned that just as my schooling neglected my unique learning style and needs as a student with ADD, so was that learning style being ignored in a course called Just and Effective Schools. In the beginning we had discussed justice and tried to define Quality as opposed to quality. However, a contradiction arose when we tried to agree upon a common truth within a class where there were the inevitably disparate views of justice and quality and where we were being graded according to the conventional competitive marking system and the professor's constructs of quality.

I approached Mike **[the Instructor]** *after class one day and requested that my paper be evaluated in a way that better suited my learning style and in a way that was lesssubjective.*

"Write up a proposal," he suggested. **[An interjection by the instructor: I made this suggestion not only to give James a choice but because I couldn't generate many options of my own using an academically trained and confined mind; said simply, I was a bit frightened and uncertain.]**

I began the proposal but halted in frustration when I realized that I was just writing another paper. I did not want to do this because I felt it was difficult for me to write well and felt speaking was a better way to express myself. The class had identified the marking system as flawed, and Mike admitted to the existence of his own artificial constructs evident in the marking scheme; I realized that the University had its own system of evaluation, tests and papers, as well. Nevertheless, in the following class, during one of our rather involved discussions about evaluation, I suggested in front of the class that we should have another method of evaluation that better suited what the students had learned and covertly served my own self-interests. A couple of chuckles and a few "yeah, why nots" were heard as Mike responded with, "Well, what do you suggest?"

I asked if the method of evaluation could be changed. Perhaps the paper and exam could be scrapped in favor of an oral presentation or class participation. Because Mike was open to suggestions the students realized that they might have the opportunity to change what they were working toward. The discussion became incredibly enthused as individual students offered various possibilities for evaluation. The first papers had already been submitted and it was quickly established that the second paper had to remain in place because of the proximity to the due date, but the final exam was open for discussion. Completely changing the evaluation process was not possible because the syllabus is considered a contract and any changes must have the unanimous approval of the students. Still, the format of the final exam was not stated in the syllabus and there existed the possibility of altering it. Not only was there opportunity for liberation from the standard form of evaluation, the collective was going to democratically decide what the format for the final exam was to be (Bergsgaard & Tyson, 2002).

"Students in our [Western] ... universities are encouraged to study philosophy, or religion, or psychology, or mysticism, or morality as if these were exclusive factors in the human mind. They are not, and the very analysis creates some of the problems faced by the professors of each. ... In the West [the study of the mind] is piecemeal; in the East total, that is, with the whole mind looking at the functions of the total mind. A mixture of feeling, analogy, reason, and intuitive vision troubles the West by its imprecision and unscientific nature. Yet the East knows more of the total [wo]man than the West yet admits to exist, and the Eastern pupil/disciple at the foot of his master, under the ancient tree or in the modern classroom, learns more of

his own mind and of All-Mind than the student of the West learns in the blinkers of analysis" (Humphreys, 1985, p. 64).

The class was not going to agree easily. Besides the few students who were content with the original method of assessment, other students suggested a take-home exam which would cover an array of topics. At this point one student took it upon himself to jump over his desk and began to write down the different ideas on the chalkboard, demonstrating just how energized the discussion was. Eventually another variable was introduced: was the exam going to be based on a mark or could it be pass or fail?

As we had already learned, an individual's definition of quality is subjective and therefore may differ for each of us. Yet the class was trying in earnest to develop an exam that would please everyone involved and ensure that it would be evaluated fairly. As well, the class contemplated the idea of the pass or fail evaluation scheme for the exam. We had discussed the concept that the educational experience was of the greatest importance and the awarding of a mark does not capture how meaningful the learning can be. Marks tend to indicate how well students parrot back the knowledge that is being taught. As the discussion continued it was apparent that many could not let go of the artificial constructs about evaluation which they had long ago been taught and had never really challenged. Some students agreed that pass/fail was an acceptable method of evaluation and even more conducive to an individual's learning; for others, using the final exam to raise their own GPAs proved to be more important than the learning experience. Although there seemed to be a collective will to challenge conventional methods of what constitutes assessing effectiveness in a classroom through a method that would be just for all, the students seemed astonished by their disagreement over what, exactly, would be a just and effective alternative. Some students advocated throwing off the traces entirely by arguing that what they were learning in the course was not quantifiable and the closest we could get to a just evaluation would be a Pass or Fail. Others seemed genuinely frightened by this prospect and defended their reluctance to abandon convention in order to maintain the GPA they had worked so hard to attain and which they believed would be their ticket into a "good" teaching position. From my perspective, we were demonstrating to ourselves the contending views on one aspect of justness and fairness and through that demonstration we became more informed not only on the subjectivity of "just and fair" but also on how immutable one's own truth seems to be.

At the conclusion of the impromptu exercise, it was agreed that the class would write a final take-home exam. As one student proposed, we were to write on what we had learned from class, how we would apply the knowledge we gained from the course in the future and were to indicate whether we wanted a letter grade or a pass/fail awarded on our exams. Only one student decided the learning experience was of the utmost value and volunteered to opt out of the final exam as long as there was a guaranteed pass in the course.

Throughout this experience students were enthused because they felt empowered at that moment by working together to bring change. Some may have recognized that they were actually using the knowledge from the course to bring change to the very course that provided the liberating moment. This was meaningful because the material was being employed in context during discussion and during the change. If the impromptu exercise never occurred perhaps the information would have had less meaning for the students. But it was a living exercise – an experiment in reality. Students were able to identify their own artificial constructs but were unable to let go of them because of the importance that evaluation has always provided in their learning. I recognized that I never tried in school and when I was graded it seemed like a game to me: A's, B's and mostly C's were awarded with as little meaning as the letters called in a Bingo hall. I always learned something in every course but the mark never spoke of what or how much I had learned. That, in this class, I had acted as a catalyst for the learning exercise to occur meant more to me than any learning experience or mark that I have ever received!

Not only was this learning experience of incredible value to me, but I observed the class recognize the contradictions of the course evaluation, use their knowledge in productive discourse and eventually recognize that they had become trapped in their own conundrum of hypocrisy. Like many educators, the class desperately wanted to solve the issue by finding something that would respect all views and allow for fair evaluation. They had to conclude that not everyone would be content with the final decision so they had to settle on something less than completely just by aiming for the middle. They could not, however, find a just and effective method to evaluate.

I believe that what my classmates made of the course experience and the exam was of far greater importance than the final mark. It asked how they as individuals would use their newly acquired knowledge in their future as classroom teachers. Stressing the importance of the subjective learning experience is easy to suggest but more difficult to explain because for such a concept to be effective it relies on individuals to conduct their own personal examination of their unique artificial constructs and to develop an ongoing process for this self-examination. I learned to do this by beginning to practice self-observation and through the inchoate recognition of my own artificial constructs. I realize that, as a teacher, I must work with artificial constructs (whether in creating rules, evaluating students or abiding by the curriculum) and I must keep focused on the subjective nature of justness and effectiveness in all of these realms. All the students will not share my truth and so it is my responsibility to acknowledge their truths in my teaching.

"I was not alone, for the divine spark which is to be found deep within each ... of us had been awakened ... no one is really alone so long as they are aware that 'It' is within them. Then, no matter where one is, no matter how profane and worldly the situation, all one needs to do is to turn and look within and one is once again united with the Source" (Ital, 1990, p. 57).

Laura Davey (personal communication, July 9, 2011): *The last month of the course truly tested our genuine understanding and acceptance of the topics covered during the course. Not only did we endeavour to change the final exam from a written component to an oral, group discussion of ideas – a format that shook many education students to their cores because it was abstract, non-linear and entirely reliant upon others – but we also came to terms with the realization that our professors were going to potentially walk off the job in order to stand up for their own Truths – and that this action could, potentially, cause harm to our end of class experience.* **[Laura is referring, here, to the possibility of a Faculty strike which created wonderful opportunities to test the ideas emerging in our class.]** *We were being faced with a battle about whether or not we truly 'bought in' and believed what we had been learning. For me, this was a big test. I had listened to professors speak for six years about how we, as teachers, were to be there, first and foremost, for our students and now, they seemed to be thinking only of themselves. I felt betrayed. After having many arguments with professors, I had the realization one day that I was basing these beliefs around artificial constructs and that I was very preoccupied about how this strike would affect me, personally; I did not see the bigger picture. What I had been learning about in Professor Bergsgaard's class was now testing me. I came to the realization that, in the grand scheme of things, in life overall, this did not matter. My life would not be put on standby. It would continue on. This realization, after several days of "angsting" and worrying about my future, was quite calming.*

As James and Laura have shared, the course – in its various manifestations – often appeared to shift student perspective on institutional learning to varying degrees, depending upon each student. Students began to question the value in what they had been taught in schools, the way in which they, as students, stood in relationship to those who "managed their learning," and the way in which their learning was evaluated. As the first incarnation of this course unfolded, that questioning enlarged to include the ways in which we go about educating teachers to become teachers, and the ways in which we prepare human beings to interact with human beings so that just and effective schooling may occur. In subsequent sections of the course, students collectively evolved their thinking on what forms the final exam would take beyond what the first class described by James accomplished. Perhaps the most perilous option, in my view, was the proposal that we conclude the course with group discussions of a final question rather than individual written work.

As often happens in the classroom, the greatest risk provided the greatest reward.

Laura Davey (personal communication, July 9, 2011): *In coming to the conclusion of the course, Professor Bergsgaard decided to give the class the option of doing an oral final exam, rather than writing a traditional university assessment. In doing this oral exam, our class would form groups – of our choosing (an integral part of the process) in order to deconstruct and demystify our thoughts from the course. [This] allowed us to* *experience genuine personal assessment. We could* **[talk]** *as much or as little as we wanted – but we had to participate and had to ensure that we helped and contributed our thoughts to the group discussion. Trying to put requirements on the discussion format would turn it into a fake experience. In group settings, some people talk a lot, others talk very little. It was this very allowance for the natural dynamics of group work that created such a positive atmosphere. Each group decided upon a topic to discuss. We did our own preparation, individually, our "studying," and we then met, at a location of our own choosing and on our own time, to discuss the theme, link it to our philosophies as individuals (and teachers), and to listen to one another's opinions and beliefs. I felt that the location and time frame was another important part of this process. It was important that the meeting place was not traditional if the group did not want it to be. Some groups met for breakfast, others met for beer. Some came to the campus, others met in a Winnipeg suburb. It was the flexibility and the trust that was given to us that gave this final assignment a genuine feel. We were not supervised. We were trusted to do our jobs. In my own experience, it was this trust that made the assignment Truthful. Doing this discussion in class, in a prescribed time frame, would have given it a sense of falseness and, I feel, that our conversation would not have been as deep or thoughtful as it was. It would have been artificial.*

In allowing us to choose our own groups, we were given the permission to choose to work with people with whom we knew we could have a genuine conversation. I was very relieved **[because]** *I know that I* **[am]** *often thrust into a leadership role,* **[and I]** *wanted to have people in my group with whom I could truly converse. I situated myself with colleagues who I had already begun discussing these ideas with, outside of class, and who I knew had taken the course seriously and had begun to do the individual work necessary in order to have a conversation that I felt was worthwhile. The unfortunate reality, in a <u>required</u> course, is that there are going to be cynics and some people who choose not to participate honestly. In speaking with some classmates, there were those who wrote certain things in* *papers, but did not necessarily believe them. They would write, or say, what they felt the professor, their 'assessor,' wanted to hear. They were still stuck in the paradigm of traditional assessment and they believed that this personal journey was complete hokum. They only cared about the grade and how it affected the GPA. They still met in groups, they still completed the assignment, but it may not have been as meaningful as it potentially could have been for them. It is their loss.*

As Laura thoughtfully details, the final exam now is an arrangement where I listen to groups of four to eight students exchange ideas over a question arising from the course for which they have no certain answer. I am amazed and humbled by the insightful, intelligent, and very thoughtful Quality conversations I am privileged to witness when the direction and flow of the discussions are not being influenced by concerns about grades, about passing or failing, or about the instructor's constructs and mythologies. Doubtless, as Laura has explained above, some students view the enterprise as demanding less physical effort than writing a two-hour exam, and very likely others still felt obliged or inclined to say what they believed I wished to hear, but as one individual said, "I've been writing tests and exams for sixteen years – I get it – now give me a chance to actually talk to other students in here without worrying about what I say to please you for a grade."

"*I* am the way, the truth and the life" [emphasis added] (John 14:6).

James Tyson (unpublished manuscript, Bergsgaard & Tyson, 2002): *While I did not get all the answers that I wanted from the course, I did come to understand how change works, how self-reflection occurs and the value of journeys – especially my own tortuous journey through school which brought me to this point. I appreciate more the opportunity to write about my thoughts and study my journey through the education system. Instead of being frustrated with the search, I learned to be content with the enjoyment derived from seeking and discovering; because I have traveled this path, I believe I will be a better teacher.*

Near The End and Next Beginning

One of the great joys in the life of any instructor is the occasion when former students return to the University simply to talk about the events of their lives and their experiences of being in the world. I wish to conclude with the following distillation (to the best of my recollection) of a recent conversation between my Self and a former Just and Effective student who is now a veteran teacher (and wishes to remain anonymous). The reader may agree that much like our lives, the conversation is one of hope and regret, joy and apprehension, thinking and feeling, behaving and learning – and as with all "events" an exact beginning and decisive ending are illusory.

Teacher (and former student): "I still remember the Just and Effective Course. I almost withdrew from that course because I was afraid I couldn't understand the ideas. It seemed like it was going to be philosophy and that has always intimidated me."

Instructor: "So why didn't you drop out?"

Teacher: "I didn't drop out because despite the fear, we seemed to be touching on deeper truths than I had explored before in University or my life. I actually started discussing these ideas with other people. The more I listened in class and talked about these ideas, the more important they became. The really exciting part, though, was when I first realized that I could comprehend the readings and the discussion. In fact, it was almost like remembering questions that I thought about years ago then abandoned because they weren't the questions discussed in school or anywhere else."

Instructor: "So you began to search for the truth of your own Self?"

Teacher: "Not right away. First, I began to see how I had been living my life out of the personal myths that I constructed or that were built on what others said about me – like I'm a good athlete, a good musician, but terrible at math. I remember one class where you asked us to meditate on the question '*Who* am I?' rather than '*What* am I?' I tried that and it was amazing how difficult it was to think something about my Self that wasn't just a label from my name to my sex to my grade point. The most awesome realization came when it hit me – I am! I am alive. ... I'd never really understood something that obvious before ... I couldn't believe how much I'd taken that fact for granted. And the instant I thought about it, I realized what a precious gift life is. Then I thought about how unpredictable it is and how it could be lost at any second. It was exhilarating and horrifying almost in the same instant."

Perhaps the most powerful proclamation a human being can make is to declare: "I am" ... attendant with that assertion may be the dread that – "I will cease to be."

Do we want to have lived the greater share of our lives without using our existence to test these assertions in the laboratories of our own minds?

Instructor: "Yes – the dilemma of being; widely recognized as a source of considerable angst and profound dread. Would you have rather not had this 'awakening?'"

Teacher: "That's like asking me whether I'd rather live out of a lie or out of the truth. No, the experience really made me appreciate the details of my life – good or bad – but I think I'm also more likely to impress upon my students how precious life is and that it shouldn't be taken as a given."

Instructor: "That's great ... at some point you might want to meditate on the question of who it was that understood that 'you are.' Most of us live what Thoreau called 'lives of quiet desperation.' We wander through existence like the beings in Plato's cave who lived amidst the shadows. It's not easy to confront those myths as you did, and it's a startling realization to suddenly and keenly understand that 'I am!'"

Teacher: "Yes, and that's when I connected 'I am' to your statement in class that 'goodness begins with being.' It was the first time I really knew deep within me that all of the wonderful and horrible things in my life happened only because I was alive. Now I was given the gift of understanding that I was alive and bringing everything else into existence because of my awareness, my consciousness. It was the most powerful experience in my life."

"Me, the one I've been so close to for as long as I can remember, myself – the door of my heart is open to me as well – to *all* of me no matter what I have done ... and please remember you do not have to be perfect, without fault to give yourself such love ... perfection never arrives" (Brahm, 2005, p. 31).

Instructor: "You may remember this (I said to the teacher as I handed her this paragraph):"

... goodness begins with being ... all that is in my life, is dependent upon being; therefore, the nurturance of being is essential to experience goodness; since the wellness and safety of my being is dependent upon yours, it is mutually beneficial to promote the essence of each. I require your being to understand and appreciate mine.

Teacher (after reading the paragraph): "I don't remember this, but I understand it. I didn't when I took the course, but I do now ... it means that the starting point for experience and awareness is my being ... nothing happens without it. Therefore, it is essential that I maintain and preserve my being. Since I need to connect to others to be happy and safe, I can also say that taking care of them is essential to me preserving my being."

Instructor: "A categorical imperative that would make Kant proud – you could come back here this year and teach the course; a better alternative may be, though, to share this with your students. You have basically constructed a fairly sound philosophy of being in the universe in which good is determined by what action preserves the wellness of your Self and other beings."

"Another time the Buddha recounted a story which made me suddenly see the supreme importance of practicing mindfulness of one's own self – that is, to protect and care for one's self, not being preoccupied about the way others look after themselves, a habit of mind which gives rise to resentment and anxiety. [In the Buddha's story], the teacher [an acrobat] instructed the pupil [of acrobatics]: 'Listen, Meda, I will watch you and you watch me, so that we can help each other maintain concentration and balance' ... but the little girl was wise and answered, 'Dear master, I think it would be better for each of us to watch ourself. To look after oneself means to look after both of us. That way I am sure we will avoid any accidents.'... If in one class, one student lives in mindfulness, the entire class is influenced" (Nhat Hanh, 1975, p. 63-64).

Teacher: "That was something I really tried to do when I first had my own class. I tried to think about the students' right to their truth, the fact that grades are constructs, the myth of the meritocracy in schools. I tired to avoid labeling students as good or bad, or smart or dumb, or even students as opposed to me as a teacher ... I really tried to keep those things in mind my first year of teaching. But students would take advantage of me, parents wanted their kids to have grades and there didn't seem to be anything I could do about students who didn't have cultural or social capital. And we're constantly being pressured to label kids with grades, with disorders, by sex. It got to be overwhelming to the point where I could barely keep up with IEPs, lesson plans, marking, meetings. And then I got married and had two kids of my own. I think I've really been drawn back into the mythos and that I'm living out of those myths as though they are truths."

Laura Davey (personal communication, July 9, 2011): *Many of us felt that we did indeed have our eyes opened to understanding the uselessness of grades; however, to completely and truly <u>unlearn</u> everything we had been taught, believed and known for several decades takes more than two to three months of a class that occurs twice a week. The process had begun for me, and for many others whom I have spoken with, but it was by no means complete. We still cared about the grade, just not nearly as much as before. We saw that there were other rewards for completing the course. Our belief system had been questioned – in a good way. Many of us were starting to see education, and our lives, differently. Thought processes had begun.*

Instructor: "The myths are always there and they're very attractive because they are easy – you don't have to think or decide, just conform. Almost every student I've known, and I include my Self, has been drawn back into the mythology of the institution; it is a natural cycle – be kind and gentle with your Self on this matter. Lapsing back into the mythos is also easy to do because there is not much in the larger society, especially media, or the institution of schooling that reminds you to stay in touch with the truth of your own being. For most of us, as soon as we become teachers, we become convinced that keeping that job is the most important thing in our life. We think about how disappointed others would be if we lost it – our parents, our friends, our partners. We think of all the material things we might lose. We fear becoming homeless, starving. More than anything, though, we fear losing our identity – the personal mythology that ensures our social position as well as our own self-image.

"Often, in forgetfulness or our [death], we become over-involved in collecting things, in attachments and possessions, in wanting to become someone special. We get involved in many of the activities of ... our ambitions, our desires, ourselves. ... If we take death as our advisor, we live each moment with the power and fullness we would give to our last endeavor on earth. ... The awareness of death provides the space of clarity in which we can understand the process of it is that we are, and who it is that dies" (Goldstein, 1976, p. 124).

When we need a job to guarantee all of those things, the next step is to avoid any risks, teach only from the curriculum, give the standardized tests, use the convenient labels – we simply become more pedantic, more inflexible, less open, and less of who we are. Just think for a moment how much of what you do is dictated by your fear of losing your job, your title, your social standing, your reputation – all of those small 'q' quality constructs that you decided constituted *what* you were, not *who* you are."

Teacher: "Those aren't things I want to think about, but I think I need to. I'm afraid that I'm becoming that unhappy burned-out teacher I swore I'd never become …"

"If we peel back our fear of conflict, we find a third layer of fear, the fear of losing identity. Many of us are so deeply identified with our ideas [and self-as-teacher] that when we have a competitive [dialectic] encounter, we risk losing more than the debate: we risk losing our sense of [our mythological] self" (Palmer, 1998, p. 38).

Instructor: "It takes work and courage to teach – it is a great risk to open up mindfully with a classroom of people – they may hurt you, they may cheat, they may complain, they may fail, they may accuse you of failing them. Those are fearsome prospects, but the greatest fear, really, truly, is not that those things will happen, but that if they do, you won't be able to handle them. You don't trust your Self anymore because you are not in touch with that Self – you are living out of the construct that you must be a predictably ordinary teacher to keep your job. You don't trust that you could say to a parent or a principal, 'You may fire me, but I will teach to human beings, not to curriculum guides or policies alone.' Think how liberating it would be if you walked into your classes every morning intending, not to preserve your job, but to promote the well-being of every one in there ... if you could trust your Self to handle what ever happens that day. My guess is that being that predictable, dogmatic teacher giving predictable boring assignments from textbooks is really at odds with that part of you that wants to connect with students in truly meaningful, creative, and useful experience. In your Self, you know that the rules, the grades, the curriculum are creating artificial barriers between you and the other people in the room, not connecting you."

Teacher: "I always thought there would be time to become that open, courageous teacher that makes the world my classroom. I see new teachers doing those things, and I almost cry when I think back to when I was like that."

Instructor: "You still are like that ... you still are that Self bringing the universe into being ... that Self hasn't disappeared and never will ... you just need to rediscover that path that leads you on the journey inward to reconnect. And I say this to you ... śāntiḥ śāntiḥ śāntiḥ"

Teacher: "Which means what?"

Instructor: "Please get back to me when you can and let me know."

Teacher: "Don't you have any more in the way of advice?"

Instructor: "I hope to distill the essence of our Just and Effective Schools course in written form; if I accomplish that, I would be honored to hear that you have read it completely."

"It is one's own ... Nature (the 'tiny point' described by Meister Eckhart) which lets one know when the time has come to begin the work of returning to unity. ... Whether seekers realize it or not, it is always they themselves who are the source of the call to set out on the journey, to search for answers, and to find out what this endless longing is" ... (Ital, 1990, p. 214).

A Fare Well from Being to Being

This discussion has not been about discovering or creating the Just and Effective school; rather, it is about the journey one takes in that direction with the awareness that the quest ends at different destinations depending upon the seeker. Even after seeming to have discovered what we thought was the grail of education, more often than not we realize that something more complete, something closer to the ideal lies further ahead, and we begin the journey anew but always mindful of where we have been and the Truths born out of that experience. I thank you for taking me along on your journey to this point and wish you constant wonder, abiding courage, and evolving wisdom as you continue in your quest.

"Deep in each ... [of us] ... is the knowledge that something knows of ... [our] ... existence" (McCarthy, 1999, p. 148).

My body is not large enough to contain my spirit, but it's a wonderful place to visit.

"Oh nobly-born, listen. Now thou art experiencing the Radiance of the Clear Light of Pure Reality. Recognize it." (Tibetan Book of the Dead, 2000, p. 95)

References

Barbour, J. (1999). *The end of time: The next revolution in physics.* New York: Oxford University Press.

Bayda, E. (2002). *Being Zen.* Boston: Shambhala.

Beck, J. C. (1993). *Nothing special: Living Zen.* San Francisco: Harper.

Benoit, H. (1990). *Zen and the psychology of transformation.* Rochester, VT: Inner Traditions International.

Bergsgaard, M., & Tyson, J. (2002). *Nexus: The birth of a democratic notion.* Unpublished manuscript, Faculty of Education, The University of Winnipeg, Winnipeg, MB.

Bhandari, D. R. (July, 2000). *Plato's concept of justice: An analysis.* Retrieved from http://www.bu.edu./wcp/papers/ anci/AnciBhan.htm

Bolte-Taylor, J. (2006). *My stroke of insight.* London, UK: Plume Books.

Bourdieu, P. (2000). Cultural reproduction and social reproduction. In R. Arum & I. R. Beattie (Eds.), *The structure of schooling: Readings in the sociology of education* (pp. 56-69). Mountain View, CA: Mayfield Publishing.

Bowles, S. (1971). Unequal education and the reproduction of the social division of labor. In J. Karabel & A. H. Halsey (Eds.), *Power and ideology in education* (pp.137-152). New York: Oxford University Press.

Brahm, A. (2005). *Who ordered this truckload of dung? Inspiring stories for welcoming life's difficulties.* Boston: Wisdom Publications.

Bryson, B. (2003). *A short history of nearly everything*. New York: Broadway Books.

Chomsky, N. (2003). *Hegemony or survival: America's quest for global dominance*. New York: Henry Holt.

Darling, D. (1996). *Zen physics: The science of death, the logic of reincarnation*. New York: HarperCollins.

Fisher, P. (1998). *Wonder, the rainbow and the aesthetics of rare experiences*. Cambridge, MA: Harvard University Press.

Freire, P. (1970). *Pedagogy of the oppressed*. New York: Continuum Publishing.

Friesen, K. (2003). The road less taken: A path to self-actualization. *The education students' anthology 2003, 29,* 8-11, 42.

Gatto-Walden, P. (2009). Living one's spirit song: Transcendent experiences in counseling gifted adults. In S. Daniels & M. M. Piechowski (Eds.), *Living with intensity* (pp. 203-224). Scottsdale, AZ: Great Potential Press.

Glasser, W. (1998). *The quality school: Managing students without coercion* (Rev. ed.). New York: Harper Perennial.

Goldstein, J. (1976). *The experience of insight: A simple and direct guide to Buddhist meditation*. Boston: Shambhala Dragon Editions.

Gregson, D., & Efran, J. S. (2002). *The tao of sobriety*. New York: St. Martin's Press.

Hamilton, S. (2009). *The lock artist*. New York: Minotaur.

Hedges, C. (2009). *Empire of illusion: The end of literacy and the triumph of spectacle*. Toronto, ON: Vintage.

Heilbroner, R. L. (1953). *The worldly philosophers: The lives, times and ideas of the great economic thinkers.* New York: Touchstone.

hooks, b. 1994. *Teaching to transgress: Education as the practice of freedom.* New York: Routledge Press.

Huber, C., & Shiver, J. (1991). *That which you are seeking is causing you to seek.* Mountain View, CA: A Center for the Practice of Zen Buddhist Meditation.

Humphreys, C. (1985*). Zen: A way of life.* Kent, UK: Hodder & Stoughton.

Ital, G. (1990). *On the way to Satori: A woman's experience of enlightenment.* Longmead, UK: Element Books.

Jackson, E. N. (1974). Afterward. In LeShan, L. (Author), *How to Meditate: A guide to self-discovery.* Boston: Back Bay Books.

Kapleau, P. (1989*). The three pillars of Zen.* New York: Anchor Books/Doubleday.

Kezwer, G. P. (1995). *Meditation, oneness and physics: A journey through the laboratories of physics and meditation.* New Delhi, India: Sterling Paperbacks.

Kohn, A. (1999). *The schools our children deserve: Moving beyond traditional classrooms and tougher standards.* Boston: Houghton Mifflin.

LeShan, L. (1974). *How to meditate: A guide to self-discovery.* Boston: Back Bay Books.

McCarthy, C. (1999). *The border trilogy: The crossing.* New York: Everyman's Library.

McTaggart, L. (2008). *The field: The quest for the secret force of the universe.* New York: Harper.

Miller, J. P. (1994). *The contemplative practitioner: Meditations in education and the professions.* Toronto, ON: OISE Press.

Nhat Hanh, T. (1975). *The miracle of mindfulness: An introduction to the practice of meditation.* Boston: Beacon Press.

Nietzsche, F. (1969). *Thus spake Zarathustra.* (R. J. Hollingdale, Trans.). New York: Penguin Books. (Original work published in 1885)

Palmer, P. J. (1998). *The courage to teach: Exploring the inner landscape of a teacher's life.* San Francisco: Jossey-Bass.

Pirsig, R. (1974). *Zen and the art of motorcycle maintenance: An inquiry into values.* New York: Bantam Books.

Reps, P. (1961). *Zen flesh, Zen bones.* New York: Doubleday.

Rhodes, R. (1986). *The making of the atomic bomb.* New York: Simon & Schuster.

Russell, P. (2000). *From science to god: The mystery of consciousness and the meaning of light.* Sausalito, CA: Lightning Source.

Sekida, K. (1985). *Zen training: Methods and philosophy.* New York: Weatherhill.

Shrewsbury, C. M. (1987). What is feminist pedagogy? *Women's Studies Quarterly, 15,* 6-14.

Suzuki, S. (1990). *Zen mind, beginner's mind.* New York: Weatherhill.

Thien-An, T. (1975). *Zen philosophy, Zen practice.* Berkeley, CA: Dharma Publishing.

Tibetan Book of the dead or: The after-death experiences of the Bardo plane according to Lama Kazi Dawa-Samdrup's English rendering. (2000). W. Y. Evans-Wentz (Ed.). New York: Oxford University Press.

Wilkinson, R., & Pickett, K. (2009). *The spirit level: Why equality is better for everyone.* London, UK: Penguin Books.

Wittgenstein. L. (2009). *Philosophical investigations* (4th ed.). UK: Wiley Blackwell.

Young, J., & Levin, B. (2002). *Understanding Canadian schools: An introduction to educational administration* (3rd ed.). Scarborough, ON: Thomson Nelson.

Appendix A

"Self Watching"

Mike Bergsgaard

Commentators writing out of a variety of theoretical frameworks acknowledge the necessity for practitioners in the professions to think more critically and introspectively about the work they do. Although early thinking on the need for individuals to reflect-in-action was focused more upon outcomes than process, recent works are more forthcoming and bold in advocating personal development as an antecedent to professional development and that individual growth results from the "practice" of reflection. The following discussion offers a unique consideration of the three conditions of "being-as-human" including the "organic impulse," the "idea-development process," and the "Self-observing"; the intention is to develop this discussion, with the emphasis on Self-observing, into an overall framework for approaching a reflective teaching practice for discussion in university education classes and as a mechanism for "praxis" or reflection in action by practicing educators.

Toward this end, I propose a reflective teaching practice intended to enhance the educator's capacity for self-observation. The framework which has been developed addresses the emergence of the "Self-observer" inherent in every individual and the means through which "observing" can be developed by practitioners working in all facets of education. In addition to elaborating upon "three conditions of being," I will offer an illustrative example of the dynamic, interactive nature of these

Reprinted in a revised form with permission from the *Journal of Educational Thought, 36* (1), 2002. Copyright: 1985/1999 by the University of Calgary.

Parts of this Appendix were also adapted, with permission, from the chapter entitled "Inward: The Journey toward Authenticity through Self-Observation" that appeared in E. Polyzoi, M. Bergsgaard, K. McCluskey, & O. Olifirovych (Eds.). (2005). *At-risk children and youth in Canada and Russia: A cross-cultural exchange for talent development* (pp. 77-92). Calgary, AB: University of Calgary Press-Gorbachev Foundation.

conditions; I hope also to offer deliberations on the benefits of teachers becoming more self-observant, and discuss possible ways to develop the process of "Self-observing."

Theoretical Framework for the Teacher Reflection Process in the Emergence of the Self-Observing

Most commonly, discussions about classrooms focus upon teachers preventing, correcting, or directing the behaviors of students whether in terms of social, academic, or affective outcomes. In the relationship to be discussed, the teacher and student will not be considered in superordinate or subordinate positions; rather, both will be viewed as equal participants in the human social-interaction that is education. Ultimately, the discussion will focus upon the benefits of the teacher coming to view interactions from the objective, non-judgmental perspective of the Self-observing.

This discussion is based upon the proposition that mental activity in human beings occurs interactively, and in some instances independently, in three forms:

Organic impulse: the fundamental process of stimulus (external or internal) and response which develops in the human being prior to the emergence of the two successive forms but also endures as long as the individual remains in a state of being. Organic impulses would include the conventional five senses, basic needs such as sustenance and shelter, and emotions such as fear, anger, loneliness, love, hate, compassion, curiosity, and jealousy.

Idea-development process: the rising of thought within the mind characterized by a capacity to recall, anticipate, discriminate, create, problem solve, choose, desire, and imagine. These ideas, to a degree difficult to ascertain, may be provoked into consciousness through the individual's volition; however, they often occur beyond the individual's capacity to control them in form or duration. Often these ideas interact with the organic impulse to create a reciprocal cycle of thought-emotion, thought-emotion. As suggested by the term "idea development," this form of mental activity often produces artificial constructs of reality with attendant emotional responses.

Self-observing: the condition of consciousness characterized by awareness, objectivity, clarity, acceptance, and being in the present as well as by the absence of opinion, preference, prejudice, and attachment. It is the emergence of the Self-observing that may be seen as a critical and integral step in the personal and professional development of teachers; it is this aspect of being that will be discussed subsequent to an elaboration upon the organic impulse, the idea-development process, and the reciprocal interplay between these two states of being.

Interplay: Organic Impulse/Idea-Development Process

Considered on a basic level, it is in the brain where organic impulses originate (Bolte-Taylor, 2006), whether in response to external sensory stimulation or as spontaneous impulses emanating from within the Self. An external stimulus may provoke the organic impulse, perhaps by being touched, perhaps by an object moving into the field of vision or perhaps by a sound; it may also be elicited by an internal source such as hunger, the rising of a memory, or the perception of danger. Although the organic impulse occurs only where there is being, the individual being did not create the impulse nor does the individual have control, in total, over the organic impulse until there is conscious intervention by the Self-observing, which will be discussed later. Even when the idea-development process begins to emanate, the way in which the individual experiences the reciprocal interaction between the organic impulse and idea-development process is axiomatic and bound by the principles of human beingness.

The idea-development process does not exist because a self willed it into being; rather, it is a process which evolves as the individual develops and matures. It is also a process which is reciprocally interactive with the organic impulse. It is because this reciprocal process of organic impulse-idea development occurs so rapidly in an axiomatic progression that we fail to discern the interplay between the two; it is because we do not recognize this interplay that we cannot recognize our limited participation as decision-makers in our lives (until we become Self observers). Quite simply, in this reciprocal state, there is no "I" with unlimited choice over emotion or thought – rather there is an "I" in a state of being. To illustrate: I am disengaged from any activity other than "sitting and thinking" of the many ideas arising from an external source – children playing outside my window – or internal source – memories, worries, desire. Now, thoughts arise of a friend who has died; the development process holds in place this subject which provokes organic impulses (in the form of feeling) which, in turn, stimulate again the idea-development process. It cannot be argued that the response elicited by the idea-development process-organic impulse interplay has been actively selected by an autonomous "me." I cannot envision my friend then choose to feel genuine sorrow. Even when I search my store-consciousness for other memories of the friend, the resulting impulses are not singly of my own doing. I may summon up a memory of tossing a football with him but the idea will not occur exactly as I "will it" either in form or in emotivity – both will emerge as shaped within me by "the principle" which drives the organic impulse and the idea development process. To explain more specifically, suppose I recall – as through a movie – me throwing the ball to the friend and him catching the ball; as this series of images unfolds, sadness wells up in me. In response, the idea development process may seize upon this memory as well as the attendant sadness and an effort is made to replay the memory; even if the replayed images recur, there will eventually be a diminution of the sadness although it is not because I chose this diminution. Indeed, there may arise a frustration when, at last, I recall the image but it evokes no emotion whatsoever. This process is not a linear, uninterrupted, and selected series of ideas and emotions; rather it is spasmodic, disjointed experience of thought or feeling which exists through my being but not through my choices until I become an Observer or Watcher of this process. Perhaps the following example of a classroom event will illustrate the idea-development process and its interaction with the organic impulse.

Classroom Scenario

During a grade-8 language arts class, a student unexpectedly gets out of his seat, walks to the door, and attempts to leave the room. The teacher asks, incredulously, "Where do you think you're going?" With an angry tone, the student responds, "I'm leaving." The teacher reacts by saying, "You're not going anywhere until you get permission. Now get back in here and sit down!" The student slams the door as he leaves the room; the teacher races after him and shouts, "Stop right where you are!" When she catches up to the student, she sees a pained look of distress on his face and in a sympathetic tone inquires whether there is a problem. More out of discomfort than anger, the student tersely explains, "I'm sick, gotta go to the washroom." At this point the teacher's fear and uncertainty give way to concern and she asks if there is anything she might be able to do.

The teacher interprets the student's behavior as a threat as soon as that behavior is inconsistent with the rules (or artificial constructs) developed for the class. This is threatening to her as the idea-development process rapidly conjures up countless possibilities: Is she losing her power, her control of the classroom? If this student challenges her authority, will the other students all get up and leave? What if the principal walks by? She believes she doesn't deserve this disrespect. She must regain control. These ideas cause her to perceive the behavior as a threat to her security and well-being. Although they are only ideas and not the reality of the event, she reacts to them with fear that she may lose control, respect, and her job because of one recalcitrant child. It is fear that provokes her to demand the student's obedience. When he refuses to comply and leaves the room, a feeling of powerlessness arises which redoubles the fear. As the teacher pursues the child, ideas occur in her mind according to her sense of justice, her desire to regain control, and her indignation over the student's behavior. These ideas sustain or intensify her anger and it is out of fear and anger, generated entirely by illusions or constructs, that she interacts with the child and commands him to stop. As soon as she sees the look of distress on the student's face, the cycle of thought-emotion is broken and the illusions from which she acted dissipate. Now, the perception of distress (organic impulse) provokes the idea that something is amiss with the child and she realizes that her reactions may have been inappropriate. It occurs to her to ask about the child's welfare to acquire the information she needs to quiet the growing sense of guilt and concern she has about the consequences for the student's inappropriate behavior. Upon hearing the student's reason for leaving the room, it becomes clear in an instant that his disregard for the rules likely resulted from his fear of being embarrassed by having to explain to his classmates the source of urgency in his departure. Projecting herself into the student's position, she now feels sympathy and compassion. Either of these organic impulses would be sufficient to prompt her to offer assistance to the student.

Especially noteworthy about this scenario are these critical points: (a) at no other place in space or time does this perception of reality exist except in the teacher's mind. In this respect, it is the teacher who has created this "reality," actual or imagined; and, (b) at no point in this scenario could it be said that the teacher was an objective, detached decision-maker, determining her behavior or her reality by deliberately selecting the thoughts and emotions she wanted to experience. She did not choose to feel fear; given a choice, she would likely have elected not to feel fear. She did not choose to confront the student but acted upon that idea which arose from experience and perception as the most probable action to protect herself. She did not choose to feel anger nor did she choose to ruminate over the impudence of the student. These emotions and ideas arose and abated without any conscious direction from her; the selection she made was according to the organic impulse in play and according to her own limited and predetermined ideas – or constructs – on right and wrong, good and bad, and power and justice (idea-development process). It is, in part, because the reciprocal interaction between the organic impulse and idea-development process occurs so rapidly in an axiomatic progression that she failed to observe the interplay between the two. Because she does not objectively observe this interplay, does not recognize herself as the "creator" of her own distress, and does not realize that her behavior is based upon a very limited repertoire of strategies or ideas for reacting to external or internal stimuli, she creates turmoil for herself and conflict with the student without "seeing" her role in the matter.

What is most remarkable in all of this is that the strongest, most stressful feelings for the teacher were not based on the simple reality of one human being leaving a room, but issued out of ideas based upon illusions or constructs that provoked emotion which provoked a further acceleration of the idea-development process. Additionally, acting out of this cycle, it was impossible for the teacher to respond appropriately to the needs of the student who is acting out of his own constructs. Had she, as the teacher, been a practiced Self-observer, she more likely would have recognized that she was feeling threatened as well as fearful and, rather than acting out of those emotions, would have responded out of a more informed sensibility so that this event would have unfolded in a less stressful way for her, and in a more caring and compassionate way toward the student and the rest of the class. If, through reflection upon previous experience, she had developed for herself the strategy of letting the fear and anger pass or responded to the student's rising from the chair with the question, "Is there anything I can do to help you?" the subsequent series of events would have been quite unlike the sequence recounted above. If she had been able to observe her thoughts and feelings as a reciprocal interplay, she may have made the connection between earlier experiences in her life and the fear she felt in this scenario. She may have come to recognize as she observed herself "reflecting and projecting" that she was constantly vigilant for threats when she was in the classroom. She may have understood that, as she taught, she also monitored other teachers, students, or administrators to assess the threat level – she may have recognized that she was generally in a state of heightened anxiety which turned instantly to fear when a threat was introduced, and then to anger when she took a measure of who was at fault and at the fates for once again putting her "at risk" whether of losing control of her students, of losing her self-respect and being humiliated, or losing her job as a teacher. As an observer or a watcher of the reflection and projection cycle, she may have come to see that action based upon reflections projected into a presumed future applied to her teaching. Just as importantly and inextricably related, she may also have come to "see" that much of her life is likely a matter of monitoring the environment, taking in sensory information, processing it in the context of her own unique constructs, then projecting possible outcomes. Reflect and project. Sense, feel, think – sense, feel, think. It is a reciprocal interplay that perhaps played out in her being countless times in a day without an awareness of how much she lived out of memories, out of projections – how much she lived out of the past and in a future that would never unfold as she imagined. And then that moment when she first becomes the observer of this drama which exists only as she creates it within the confines of her own mind – that instant may be for her that absolutely stunning realization of how little time most of us spend living in the present reality, in the immediacy of life and in control of our own being. It is at that moment, too, when she becomes better prepared and positioned to guide her students into an awareness, not only of the constructs dictating their actions, but also of the power they have to generate alternative strategies which may be healthier and more productive.

What requires elaboration at this point is the role of the Self-observing in extricating ourselves from the cyclical, unexamined interplay between the organic impulse and the idea-development process. Understanding of this point is crucial to awareness of how teachers interact with students; however, it is an examination or observation they rarely make because of the rapidity of the interplay and because they have not been trained to observe themselves.

Self-Observing

What does it mean to become Self-observing and how can this way of being lead teachers to more accurate perceptions of reality and to behaviors which are more compassionate and based less on illusory constructs? With the emergence of Self-observing, the individual comes into possession of a process through which he or she may watch the organic impulse and the idea-development process; in other words, one now understands the power the Self has in determining outcomes. To become Self-observing one turns one's gaze inward.

When Self-observing, we extricate ourselves from the illusionary constructs generated upon perceiving a student rise from a desk, and recognize, that on a fundamental level, the event is a matter of one human being walking from a room – nothing more and nothing less. The teacher may feel threatened by the behavior but in the process of observing this threat, she is aware that it is arising out of illusory scenarios which the idea-development process is rapidly constructing to trigger organic impulses in the form of emotion. As an observer of this process, she allows the ideas to arise and dissipate and emotional responses become just as ephemeral. When she does respond to the perceived event, it is according to the pure reality of the matter and not in response to an idea and an emotion of which she has only limited awareness.

How do teachers become observers of themselves? Without process and practice, it is very difficult to arrange the timely appearance of this Self-observing. One cannot say with any true expectation, "I shall spend the next ten minutes in uninterrupted observation of my Self by my Self." I may promise myself that the next time a student breaks a rule, I will remain the objective observer and avoid becoming entrapped in the organic-impulse/idea-development cycle, but most likely, without practice in the interim, I will slip into the cycle as naturally and unmindfully as always.

Strategies for Self-Observation

Although perhaps not essential, it may be argued that aspiring practitioners of Self-observation would benefit greatly from understanding thoroughly the concepts and dynamics put forth in the foregoing discussion of the organic-impulse/idea-development cycle, and the observing Self. Once we understand the nature of each condition of being, we are much more likely to recognize organic impulses as the emotions and feelings that are experienced and shared by all of us. The idea-development process must be acknowledged as a wonderful mechanism for creativity, divergent thinking, problem solving, and imagination; however, it is also the process through which we worry, develop countless angst-inducing scenarios, create stereotypes and biases, make assumptions and generate unwarranted feelings of fear, anger, loneliness, and despair. To recognize the illusory nature of the products of the idea-development process is to locate ourselves in a perspective which is far more likely to allow us to observe the true nature of these constructs and the reciprocal interplay with the organic impulse. To accept that there is the human capacity to observe our thoughts and feelings is to give us hope that we can better ensure our own well-being, to allow us to interact more thoughtfully with others, and to pique the curiosity we all have but need aroused to explore our own interiors. If we, at this juncture, can envision one of our goals as the nurturing of the Self-observing, then perhaps we can offer the following strategies as possibilities for beginning this quest.

Contemplative Practice

In *The Contemplative Practitioner*, John Miller (1994) advocates the practice of meditative forms to foster Self-observation, or in his words, "contemplative awareness" from which "we see things as they are in the here and now ... [becoming] ... totally attuned to what is happening in the moment" (p. 2). Miller also stresses the value in discerning between the constructed reality of the idea-development process, which he terms "ego chatter," and pure reality when he writes that: "... we learn that we can witness our thoughts rather than simply run on 'automatic pilot,' reacting unconsciously to our thoughts" (p. 27). Miller suggests further that through "witnessing our thoughts" or Self-observing, we experience being as "unmediated awareness ... characterized by openness, a sense of relatedness ... where we can see our students as [teachers] who with their directness can awaken us if we remain open" (p. 25). In the classroom scenario detailed earlier, had the teacher been observing not only classroom events, but her own thoughts (or "ego chatter") generated by the idea-development process and feelings arising out of those thoughts, she would have been more capable of acting out of clarity and the awareness that, on a fundamental level, all that had actually transpired was another human being leaving a room. Recognizing that as being the situation, the teacher may have been less concerned about control issues, rule breaking, and personal consequences and more open to the needs of the student and a healthier way of interacting with him. Although functional when mindfully utilized, constructs such as rules, authority, "the teacher," and "the student" are merely constructs in the form of labels or abstract concepts. The contemplative practitioner brings this awareness to the interaction we call education and can be more thoughtful and flexible in working with the people whom we may label as students but who become our teachers when we open ourselves to that possibility.

Journaling

The power of journaling to come to know oneself at an intimate level has been widely used for many years in disciplines such as psychology and English, and more recently within the field of education. Progoff (1975) introduced the concept of the "Intensive Journal" technique whereby, through writing about one's life, a person comes to understand that there is a connective thread that has been forming beneath the surface during the individual's entire lifetime. Greene (1995) writes, "A reflective grasp of our life stories and of our ongoing quests that reaches beyond where we've been depends upon our ability to remember things past. It is against the backdrop of those things remembered and the meanings to which they give rise, that we grasp and understand what is now going on around us" (p. 20). Connelly and Clandinin (1988) wrote about journal keeping as a tool for "reflection-on-action." A teacher, through journaling, can note classroom activities, his/her behaviors, and observations of specific students and groups of children, as well as the ways in which a teacher interacts with individuals or groups according to race, gender, class, or other student characteristics. Again, to call upon the teacher in the classroom scenario, many educators who experience such an interaction, albeit relatively minor, find it difficult to "let go" of the matter. It would not be unusual for the teacher to replay the event as real across an entire evening and to experience repeatedly the thoughts and emotions that were conjured up by her own idea-development process in the first place. In some instances, perhaps the teacher formulates a new plan to "put the child in his place," or a new rule to preclude the recurrence of a similar situation. As an alternative, however, journaling can be a cathartic experience through which one begins to observe one's own emotions and feelings, to enlarge the event to include not only the focus-student but the entire class and, when practiced mindfully, release the teacher from the unexamined cycle of thought and emotion.

Breathing Techniques

Breathing Techniques can provide a process for enabling teachers to become more Self-observant. In *Time Shifting*, Rechtschaffen (1996) suggests that harried teachers may rediscover the more natural rhythms of their bodies and reconnect with authentic reality simply by using breaks from teaching (e.g., recess, lunch) to observe themselves breathing slowly and deeply (p. 85). Breathing techniques as a means of quieting the mind are a cornerstone of many traditions of meditation which may be practiced at work or at home.

The Relaxation Response (Benson, 1976) is a seminal work in which a Western physician details the importance of breathing techniques in meditation practices in Judaic, Christian,

Buddhist, Sufi, and Yogic traditions and reports upon medical research confirming the value of meditation in reducing anxiety, stress, and related disease.

Based upon a nexus of Eastern and Western thinking, Benson (1976) identified four key components in the relaxation process: (a) a quiet environment; (b) a mental device, such as a work or sound which is repeated; (c) a comfortable position; and (d) a passive attitude which Benson describes as "... perhaps the most important element in eliciting the Relaxation Response" (p. 160). This passive attitude allows emotions and ideas to pass through one's mind without attachment to enable the Self to watch the Self.

When the ideas proposed by Rechtschaffen and Benson are coupled, we are offered a model through which teachers can "practice" watching ideas and thoughts rise and fall outside the seemingly frenetic confines of the classroom; as they learn to watch the interplay between the organic impulse and idea-development process, they see more clearly the etiological relationship as it plays out in its unique way in each of us and also the nebulous and ephemeral nature of most thoughts and feelings. When this practised awareness of breathing and the Self is brought forward into the classroom, what appeared to be a charged, frantic, and chaotic environment can be viewed by the objective but compassionate observer as individual human beings all interacting out of their own needs in ways that make sense to each according to the principles of their own constructs.

Meditation

Forms of meditation have existed in both eastern and western cultures and religions for centuries. The use of meditation is a way for pre-service and practicing teachers to tap into the mindfulness and awareness that leads to the Self-observing.

In his work on meditation, *Zen Training: Methods and Philosophy*, Sekida (1985) uses different terminology but describes clearly not only the cyclical interplay between the organic impulse and the idea-development process, but also details the instructive value of this interaction to human development; he also explains the role of the Self-observing in bringing new options into the idea-development process. It is Sekida's (1985) position that all that is observed by the Self is integrated into "the stream of consciousness and passed along with new impression" (p.112), to what we have referred to as the idea-development process and organic impulse. Sekida devotes a large part of his book to the importance of posture and breathing in practicing Self-observation and provides considerable research data on the effects of consistent meditative practice. Another contribution made by Sekida is his emphasis upon the necessity for us to accept without partiality or judgment the equal value of the organic impulse, the idea-development process, and the Self-observing in our unfolding as human beings.

Dr. John Harvey (1994), whose medical practice focuses upon children with learning disabilities and attention deficit disorders, describes breathing-meditation as a process through "which ... we cultivate the ability to watch our thoughts without necessarily reacting to them ... [or] ... getting caught up in our mental melodrama ... we can simply notice and label the current activity of the mind ... acknowledge it with present centered awareness, and let it go" (p. 17). Applied to the classroom scenario, the teacher notices the student rising from his desk, watches the threat-inducing event pass through her mind, acknowledges it is not the reality of the moment, and then lets go of it. Subsequent to this fleeting process of observation, the teacher has the option of acting on the basis of reality rather than illusion.

Yoga

The art of yoga is 5,000 years old and was first put into written form 2,500 years ago (Zebroff, 1971). Lilias Folan (1994), widely recognized in North America as an expert in yoga, defines it as "the science and study of the self" (p. 26). She also argues that "breathing and relaxation techniques are at the core of yoga practice ... [and that] ... you can learn to quiet the mind by quieting the breath" (p. 27). Through the practice of yoga, we again have available a means to learn to study our own interiors; in doing so, we gradually learn more about what events or behaviors in others elicit what particular thoughts and emotions in our Selves. With this awareness, we can affect interventions in some interplays between organic impulses and the idea-development process and we can also learn to find harmony with situations or behaviors which cause us discomfort. For instance, as teachers dealing with a parent whom we believe to be making unreasonable demands or unwarranted accusations, we can watch the words of the parent reaching our ears, entering into our thinking, and evoking emotion. We can see the enormous control we actually have over our thoughts and feelings as we let each pass in its normal course. When we do respond, it is less likely to be out of fear, anger, or revenge but out of objectivity, clarity, and equanimity.

Visualization/Relaxation Techniques

There are many strategies for learning visualization and relaxation techniques. In "Creative Visualization," Gawain (1994) asserts that "simply having an idea or thought ... [and] ... holding it in your mind" (p.112) becomes the basis upon which subsequent action is taken. According to Gawain, an effective method for replacing negative, hostile thoughts about another (in our example, a student) is to practice relaxation techniques such as those offered by Benson; rather than repeating a sound, however, one envisions communicating with one's "antagonist" in "an open, honest, and harmonious way" (p. 109). In this fashion, one is infusing the organic-impulse/idea-development cycle with a new, larger, and, hopefully healthier perspective and disrupting the negative cycle of fear and aggression toward the student. Gawain emphasizes the need for sincerity in this process as well as the value in repeating the visualization several times daily. Ideally, the next interaction with the student would be guided by a more positive, open attitude on the part of the teacher with an attendant change in the behavior of the student.

Conclusion

In the foregoing discussion, we have considered several methods through which Self-observing may begin to be experienced by students in education classes, practicing teachers, and teacher educators. This does not imply an exhaustive list. It is important that as educators we have some experience with these strategies before we presume to facilitate the emergence of the observing Self in our students. Courses in contemplative observation, journaling, yoga, and meditation would no doubt enhance the quality and sincerity with which faculty introduce the suggested methods in university classrooms. Journaling, or the process of writing to one's Self, is a reflective practice through which we may gain insights into how the organic-impulse/idea-development cycle works in our unique selves. With the benefit of these insights, we are more likely to develop alternative responses to student behavior and other events in the classroom environment (including teaching methodologies). Journaling and meditation courses are offered through local colleges, professional development activities, and retreat centers. Courses on various forms of visualization and relaxation techniques are also offered weekly in our communities.

To teach and to learn are human enterprises through which we develop understanding not only about ourselves but others. It is through the emergence of the Self-observing that we bring clarity, authenticity, and reality to our teaching and learning, not only in the classroom but also in the world outside the classroom door. We must be ever vigilant that developing the Self-observing is a never-ending process of growth and we are all at different stages of growth. We cannot frighten, cajole, nor coerce the Self-observing into emergence in our Selves or others; rather we must accept the point where we are in our lives. This point is not a matter of right or wrong, but merely our unique place in our development. It is when we acquire tolerance, awareness, and acceptance of the unique place that we each occupy that we can begin to collectively move forward, helping one another while nurturing the growth of our own special selves.

References

Benson, H . (1976). *The relaxation response.* New York: Avon.

Bolte-Taylor, J. (2006). *My stroke of insight: A brain scientist's personal journey.* London, UK: Penguin Books.

Connelly, M. F., & Clandinin, J. D. (1988). *Teachers as curriculum planners: Narratives of experience.* Toronto, ON: OISE Press.

Folan, L. (1994). Yoga. In L. Blumenfeld (Ed.), *The big book of relaxation* (pp. 107-122). New York: The Relaxation Company.

Gawain, S. (1994). Creative visualization. In L. Blumenfeld (Ed.), *The big book of relaxation* (pp. 107-122). New York: The Relaxation Company.

Greene, M. (1995). *Relaxing the imagination.* San Francisco: Jossey-Bass.

Harvey, J. (1994). Meditation. In L. Blumenfeld (Ed.), *The big book of relaxation* (pp. 7-24). New York: The Relaxation Company.

Miller, J. P. (1994). *The contemplative practitioner: Meditations in education and the professions.* Toronto, ON: OISE Press.

Progoff, I. (1975). *At a journal workshop.* New York: Dialogue House Library.

Rechtschaffen, S. (1996). *Time shifting.* New York: Doubleday.

Sekida, K. (1985). *Zen training: Methods and philosophy.* New York: Weatherhill.

Zebroff, K. (1971). *Volume I, The ABC of yoga.* Vancouver, BC: Forbez Enterprises.

Appendix B

From: "In Search of Lost Prizes: Big Dreams and Promises to Keep"

Mike Bergsgaard and Ken W. McCluskey

When considering the career paths and lives of our former high school classmates, it seems as though both were surprisingly predictable in several ways. Essentially, those high school students whom we remembered as coming from upper socio-economic backgrounds and homes where the parents were active in their children's lives and in the community held more prestigious jobs today. The in-group in high school was still the in-group decades later, and those who had languished near the bottom of the social ladder in school were almost uniformly in lower-paying and less highly regarded occupations (Bergsgaard, 2005).

Of course, there were a few exceptions. There almost always are, and those exceptions have long been used as evidence that rich kids can come to a bad end and poor kids can rise to the pinnacle of our society. But despite these aberrations, our own "deep attention" to the "everyday" brought us to the conclusion that wealth begets wealth and poverty predicts poverty. Affluent people network with other affluent people, while those living in poverty tend to interact with others of similar socio-economic status (which we mean to include household income, the education level of parents/guardians, and the occupation of parents).

Indeed, this "birds of a feather flock together" tendency is a much-advertised advantage and rationale of and for private schools – making connections that will be useful later in life. Children enrolled in private schools, particularly in elite institutions with high entrance requirements and equally high

Reprinted in a revised form with permission from ICIE. The original chapter, of the same title, appeared in L. Sokal & K. W. McCluskey (Eds.). (2013). *Community connections: Reaching out from the ivory tower* (pp. 206-240). Ulm, Germany: International Centre for Innovation in Education.

tuition fees, are immediately positioned to form bonds with other children standing to inherit something that will serve them well for a life-time: "social capital."

Hagan (1999) defined social capital as "the creation of capabilities through socially structured relations between individuals in groups" (p. 333). In the context of education, those parents who have positive structured relations – not only with their children but also with the educators of their children – have the capability to advocate more successfully and actively on their children's behalf within the school system. This holds true not only because the parents or primary caregivers are familiar with how schools work, but also because they know, in a very literal sense, those who work in the schools. Parents who lack familiarity with the dynamics of the system and with those who are employed in it have limited ability to represent their children's interest and affect their achievement (Bergsgaard & Sutherland, 2003).

In his critical work on social capital, *Bowling Alone*, Putnam (2000) has offered quantitative data to support his observations that, in the latter part of the 20th century, social capital in general plummeted as Americans began disconnecting themselves from voluntary community associations. His metaphor – of more and more people bowling alone rather than in leagues – captures the fact that something has been lost as individuals have distanced themselves from family, neighbors, friends, community, and democratic structures. Putnam stressed that it is critically important to revive the sense of American community.

At first sight, such a revival would be logical and universally beneficial. Taking a different perspective, however, an imbalance of social capital in the process subtly paves the way for inequality to continue to raise its ugly head. Reviving community networks and connections will not offer the same outcomes or opportunities for all. In interpreting Bourdieu's (2000) conceptualization, Dika and Singh (2002) have argued that because social capital consists of connections and social obligations, it can often be converted directly into economic capital. If that is true, we can see how the child who enters school with interactive parents, healthy cohort links, networks with the larger community, and nascent bonds with the supposedly "best and the brightest" is far more likely to acquire the social capital that can later be parlayed into social position and financial success for her or himself and future offspring. It is not the child's merit or industry alone that factor into school success; the socio-economic status of the child's parent is a factor. And it is not only SES, it is also the social capital factored into the relationship the child and parents have with the school. To further clarify and perhaps compound the matter, we concur with Bourdieu (2000) that success in schools is also dependent upon the extent to which the child's cultural capital coincides with the school, if we define cultural capital as those tangibles and intangibles valued by the dominant sector of a society (Bergsgaard, 2005). Wilkinson and Pickett (2009) offer compelling evidence that "Children do better if their parents have higher incomes and more education themselves, and they do better if they come from homes where they have a place to study, where there are reference books and newspapers, and where education is valued" (p. 105). Moreover, if we consider a recently proposed form of capital, "mythological capital" (K. Venema, personal communication, May, 2011), it may be readily understandable that very few children situated on the margins will perform well in schools. We may define mythological capital in the following way: the power or capacity to improve one's circumstance or influence the status of others through constructs conferred by institutions or societal norms. To some extent, these may be considered the intangible aspects of cultural capital but, more specifically, may be named as titles, degrees, certificates, credentials, and honors.

One is left to wonder where "intelligence" really does begin to matter in schooling, but one also begins to sense that the "equal chance" homily is in itself the stuff of dreams. It seems abundantly clear to us that a first grader from a home where parents enjoy a high level of socio-economic status and where this child is endowed with cultural capital and social capital will have opportunities that will be denied to classmates less favorably positioned in society. Perhaps at this point, the reader would wish to examine these contentions in the context of his or her own experience as we did and may arrive at these questions which arose for us.

If it is not merit and industry alone that predict educational outcomes and social status, why doesn't everyone in school and everyone in our society know this? Why don't those who have it share their stores of cultural and social capital? In Lin's (1999) view, social capital can be seen as an investment or mechanism used by the upper class to preserve and reproduce their group's dominant position in society. So, while some definite positives will result if more people become involved in philanthropic service clubs, not every child's parents will have the chance to become members of such clubs. And if they do become members, they must know how to talk, how to dress, and how to display cultural capital in a manner that will secure their social affiliations. Said simply, although it may be "radically chic" to invite a gang member to a $500 a plate charity dinner, that gang member is not likely to have the language, the titles, the degrees, the "graces," and the nuanced urbanity that will secure a position in that social network any more than a city's affluent would be able to find a comfortable place in a street gang.

Indeed, it is imperative that social, cultural, and mythological capital are sequestered and protected by those who have it. Furthermore, essential to preserving this power and position held by the dominant group is the denial of access to social capital to the vast majority of children in our schools and members of our society. In the same way certain elite groups secret, hoard, and protect financial capital, they also secret, hoard, and protect social capital to give themselves an advantage over others. It's interesting to see how often the most strident calls for educational reform come from hard-line descendants of privilege, who envision as "proper" any reforms that are shaped in their image, perpetuate the status quo, and further disadvantage and punish the victims of inequality. Clearly, in education, social capital affords benefits to some students while at the same time disadvantaging others who do not possess it in the form valued by the school. The key to maintaining this hegemony is to not discuss it, particularly with the children and teachers working in our schools. Better to let the best and brightest believe they truly are doing it all on their own merit and let the worst and the dimmest live with the lie that their plight is the consequence of genetic misfortune. And now, of course, we trust that the reader is forming some thoughts as well, about why we are not encouraged in school to "reflect" upon what it is we are doing whether as a student or a teacher.

Even if it was never discussed, even if reflection was not encouraged, however, most of us, from the earliest days in school, had a sense the playing field was dramatically tilted. We learned a lot more in the first grade than the teacher taught us. Before we as students settled into our first desk in our first classroom, some of our parents had already had conversations with administrators and teachers to establish that critical conduit between the home and the school. Some children had already developed strong social bonds with other children through neighborly interactions or mutual participation in community activities – team sports, various youth groups, religious activities, or interactions with the children of parental acquaintances.

We need not be in school long or to reflect deeply to understand that one of the "everyday" things the system does is to group us. We're placed in discrete grades and classrooms. Within each grade, we're further divided: Fast readers become "bluebirds" and slow ones become "mud turtles." Because these forms of mythological capital seem to make sense to the teacher, the overt and conspicuous sorting mechanisms are generally accepted by parents and students alike.

On a more subtle level, though, another more covert form of grouping is going on. There are groups or individuals whom the teacher seems to prefer over others. There are children who are obedient and those who cause problems. There are children everyone seems to like and those no one dares like. There are some who seem absolutely delighted to be in school and others who appear to be enduring a long-term sentence in a penal colony. There are kids whose parents have a way of showing up for everything from PTA to the school dance, and kids who seem not to have parents or other living kin. There are students who are given more challenging work and others who labor over what seems to be the same assignment every day. There are groups that leave the room for enrichment and those that leave for remedial work. Perhaps most importantly, there are students who get good grades and those who get poor grades. Even back then, we would have been willing to bet our allowances that the kids getting good grades were not the "parentless" ones doing assembly-line academics and appearing to view school with the same loathing the rest of us had reserved for flu shots. We all knew that different kids in different groups got different treatment – and nobody said a thing.

Hopefully, by this point, the reader can see enough of his or her own experience in what we are saying to be interested in what others have observed about unequal education in our schools. For example, almost any issue of *Reclaiming Children and Youth* will illustrate how unfair our society can be for economically disadvantaged, culturally different, or otherwise marginalized students.

Of course these children often have cultural and social capital in their immediate neighborhood or family but not of the sort highly prized in schools. In their seminal research on social capital, Horvatt, Weininger, and Lareau (2003) offered compelling evidence that, while "middle class" parents were able to mobilize other parents and call upon professionals to respond to issues in school affecting their children, "working class" parents relied more upon relatives without school affiliations and the school itself for support.

Further to the power of cultural capital, Torrance has expressed the view that "Our educational system often penalizes children who are raised with different values and attitudes from those found in the dominant culture" (Torrance, Goff, & Satterfield, 1998, p. 1). While the U.S. Department of Education (1993) has long espoused the notion that talent in abundance can be found in students from all economic levels and cultural groups, Aboriginal students are much less likely to have their abilities recognized and nurtured than their non-Aboriginal counterparts (Callahan & McIntire, 1994). Indeed, another governmental report flagged this under-representation by showing that while the national average for student participation in enrichment programs in American schools was 8.8 percent, it was only 2.1 percent for students of Indian/Alaska Native descent (U.S. Department of Education, 1991). Similar trends have also been observed for children from other minority groups. To illustrate, in a comprehensive cross-cultural study conducted by Sisk (1993), not a single African American, Hispanic, or Navajo student in four locations initially met the requirements for inclusion in a gifted program. None were even nominated by their teachers. Following three years in a program stressing motivation, however, it eventually turned out that some 50 percent of them met the criteria.

Although studies of this type have raised awareness to some degree and led to the creation of certain culturally sensitive enrichment interventions that acknowledge diverse forms of cultural capital, unbiased programming remains the exception rather than the rule. Pockets of enlightenment exist, but they are still relatively few and far between.

As we reflect upon our inequities in the classroom as well as the inequality in our world, the seemingly age-old nature versus nurture controversy may come to mind: Are we as humans what we are due to innate genetic predispositions or because of environmental factors and learning? Are those doing well in school possibly succeeding simply because they inherited exceptional "intelligence" along with the necessary capital? Put another way, do they have social and cultural capital because they and their parents ARE the best and the brightest?

There are undoubtedly some inborn differences that allow certain individuals to do things that others cannot, and vice versa. Of course, the realities are rapidly changing as geneticists become more and more able to affect and alter what were, until now, immutable innate characteristics. The point remains, though, that where there is human interaction, there is still opportunity; educators can push the limits and stretch the boundaries of learning by providing enrichment, encouragement, and environmental opportunity for all students. Shenk (2010) has put it well in his discussion of "dynamic development" by asserting that "Your life is interacting with your genes" (p. 27) and that "Talent is not a thing; it's a process" (p. 8). In other words, the child reading, playing a guitar, kicking a soccer ball, discussing political views, networking on-line, and doing science experiments in the basement has a life interacting differently with his/her genes than a child who can't read, can't play an instrument, can't afford sports, can't access a computer, and is more fearful of science than what might be in the basement. Perhaps just as importantly, a child who has been taught to value education, and who has been taught to work diligently under the tutelage of a teacher or parent, has gained cultural capital that will yield both immediate and life-long benefits (in contrast to a child whose parents see no value in schooling and doubt it did them any more good than it could do for their children).

The well-known quotation from Edison, "Genius is one percent inspiration and ninety-nine percent perspiration," illustrates the importance of hard work in developing talent. Shenk (2010) has offered other examples: Ted Williams said his hitting prowess resulted from super discipline and that "Nothing except practice, practice, practice will bring out that ability" (p. 5); Mozart wrote to his father that "Nobody has devoted so much time and thought to composition as I" (p. 57); and Einstein remarked "It's not that I'm so smart. It's just that I stay with problems longer" (p. 113). So the good news is that a child who may not be succeeding and who may not have a strong work ethic may do a reversal on the road to failure if given reason to begin working with the hope that "perspiration" might make the future brighter and the moment more enjoyable. In other words, where there has been a severe imbalance in the distribution of cultural capital, we can strive to tilt the field back to the favor of equality-in-opportunity – opportunity which many marginalized students simply do not have. It is more difficult to work hard when there is no joy in the labor and no reward in the result. It is harder to be all that you can be when there is no one interested in searching for your talents, no one to mentor and guide you along, and no money for a piano, sports equipment, art supplies, or community drama classes. For many young people, the injustice and inequality are distressingly palpable and these children could not fail to feel some frustration because too many of their teachers fail to notice the inequities in "everyday" life.

Speaking from personal experience gained through our youth-focused projects, we've been amazed by what marginalized young people have been able to accomplish when given half a chance. Certainly, once their talents were identified and nurtured, many of these "lost prizes" turned their lives around in rather dramatic fashion (Bergsgaard, Land, & Myles, 2003; McCluskey, Baker, Bergsgaard, & McCluskey, 2003; McCluskey, Baker, & McCluskey, 2005). In our various initiatives, we've employed approaches drawn from programs such as Life Space Crisis Intervention (Long, Wood, & Fecser, 2001), Response Ability Pathways (Brendtro & du Toit, 2005), Developmental Audit (Brendtro & Shahbazian, 2004), Circle of Courage (Brendtro, Brokenleg, & Van Bockern, 2002), Creative Problem Solving (Treffinger, Isaksen, & Stead-Dorval, 2006), and mentoring (Lamoureux, McCluskey, Wiebe, & Baker, 2008). Without doubt, these strength-based interventions have had a very tangible (and measurable) positive impact in terms of reclaiming large numbers of so-called at-risk individuals (McCluskey, with Baker, Bergsgaard, Glade, Lamoureux, McCluskey, & Wiebe, 2012).

It could be argued, too, that the inequality in educational opportunity not only reflects our larger society, but also, as Bowles (1971) has argued, that schools are intended to reproduce the stratification in our society if not the hegemony of our planet. The parallels between groups in schools and the striations of our world are hard to miss if one is attentive; and, just as students in high school rarely cross the demarcations between "cliques," so their parents maintain affiliations according to income levels, careers, and education. How often do adults from favorable circumstances leave the comfort of their suburban homes to connect with those living in inner-city poverty? Probably about as frequently as inner-city youth foray into ritzy neighborhoods to hang with the kids there. This is the preservation and the reproduction of social capital (Bergsgaard, 2005). Even when caring, philanthropic types give to help the unfortunate, it is often a case of noblesse oblige rather than the result of genuine understanding. To borrow from a colleague and relative, "Everyone is going to save the day, but no one stays the night" (McCluskey & McCluskey, 2012).

References

Bergsgaard, M. (2005). White lies: Schooling and "social capital." *Our Schools/Our Selves, 14* (2), 87-106.

Bergsgaard, M., Land, R., & Myles, E. (2003). The prism project: Colors in the dark. In K. W. McCluskey & A. M. Mays (Eds.), *Mentoring for talent development* (pp. 87-102). Lennox, SD: Reclaiming Youth International.

Bergsgaard, M., & Sutherland, D. (2003). Hidden currency: Social and cultural capital in inner-city schools. In D. Sutherland & L. Sokal (Eds.), *Resiliency and capacity building in inner-city learning communities* (pp. 189-206). Winnipeg, MB: Portage & Main Press.

Bourdieu, P. (2000). Cultural reproduction and social reproduction. In R. Arum & I. R. Beattie (Eds.), *The structure of schooling: Readings in the sociology of education* (pp. 56-69). Mountain View, CA: Mayfield Publishing.

Bowles, S. (1971). Unequal education and the reproduction of the social division of labor. In J. Karabel & H. Halsey (Eds.), *Power and ideology in education* (pp. 137-152). New York: Oxford University Press.

Brendtro, L. K., Brokenleg, M., & Van Bockern, S. (2002). *Reclaiming youth at risk: Our hope for the future* (Rev. ed.). Bloomington, IN: Solution Tree.

Brendtro, L. K., & du Toit, L. (2005). *Response ability pathways*. Capetown, South Africa: Pretext Publishers.

Brendtro, L. K., & Shahbazian, M. (2004). *Troubled children and youth: Turning problems into opportunities*. Champaign, IL, Research Press.

Callahan, C. M., & McIntire, J. (1994). *Identifying outstanding talent in American Indian and Alaska Native students*. Washington, DC: U.S. Department of Education (Javits Gifted and Talented Education Program, Office of Educational Research and Improvement).

Dika, S. L., & Singh, K. (2002). Applications of social capital in educational literature: A critical synthesis. *Review of Educational Research, 72* (1), 31-61.

Hagan, J. (1999). Social capital in crime. In F. T. Cullen & R. Agnew (Eds.), *Criminological theory: Past to present* (pp. 332-339). Los Angeles: Roxbury Publishing.

Horvat, E. R., Weininger, E. B., & Lareau, A. (2003). From social ties to social capital: Class differences in the relations between schools and parent networks. *American Educational Research Journal, 40* (2), 319-351.

Lamoureux, K., McCluskey, K. W., Wiebe, A., & Baker, P. A. (Eds.). (2008). *Mentoring in a Canadian context*. Winnipeg, MB: Institute of Urban Studies, The University of Winnipeg.

Lin, N. (1999). Building a network theory of social capital. *Connections, 22* (1), 28-51.

Long, N. J., Wood, M. M., & Fecser, F. A. (2001). *Life space crisis intervention: Talking with students in conflict* (2nd ed.). Austin, TX: pro•ed.

McCluskey, C.I., & McCluskey, K.C. (2012). *Lost prizes: Reclaiming at-risk gifted youth.* Paper presented at the Conference of the African Federation for the Gifted and Talented, Nairobi, Kenya.

McCluskey, K. W. (with P. A. Baker, M. Bergsgaard, L. Glade, K. Lamoureux, A. L. A. McCluskey, & A. C. Wiebe). (2012). *Lost prizes: Manitoban and international initiatives to identify and develop the talents of at-risk populations.* Winnipeg, MB: Manitoba Education Research Network.

McCluskey, K. W., Baker, P. A., Bergsgaard, M., & McCluskey, A. L. A. (2003). Interventions with talented at-risk populations with emotional and behavioural difficulties. In D. Montgomery (Ed.), *Gifted and talented children with special educational needs: Double exceptionality* (pp. 168-185). London, England: David Fulton Publishers.

McCluskey, K. W., Baker, P. A., & McCluskey, A. L. A. (2005). Creative problem solving with marginalized populations: Reclaiming lost prizes through in-the-trenches interventions. *Gifted Child Quarterly, 49* (4), 330-341.

Putnam, R. (2000). *Bowling alone: The collapse and revival of American community.* New York: Simon and Schuster.

Shenk, D. (2010). *The genius in all of us. Why everything you've been told about genetics, talent, and IQ is wrong.* New York: Doubleday.

Sisk, D. (1993). *Systemic training educational programs for under-served pupils (Project Step-UP)*. Washington, DC: U.S. Department of Education.

Torrance, E. P., Goff, K., & Satterfield, N. B. (1998). *Multicultural mentoring of the gifted and talented*. Waco, TX: Prufrock Press.

Treffinger, D. J., Isaksen, S. G., & Stead-Dorval, K. B. (2006). *Creative problem solving: An introduction* (4th ed.). Waco, TX: Prufrock Press.

U.S. Department of Education (1991). *National education longitudinal study (NELS:88) on gifted and talented education*. Washington, DC: Author.

U.S. Department of Education (1993). *National excellence: The case for developing America's talent*. Washington, DC: Author.

Wilkinson, R., & Pickett, K. (2009). *The spirit level: Why equality is better for everyone*. London, UK: Penguin Books.